I0123460

Cosmic Science
Of The
Ancient Masters

Professor Hilton Hotema

ISBN: 978-1-63923-119-5

Printed February 2022

Cover Art By: Paul Amid

Published and Distributed By:
Lushena Books
607 Country Club Drive, Unit E
Bensenville, IL 60106
www.lushenabks.com

ISBN: 978-1-63923-119-5

Table of Contents

Prologue
Myth Or Truth?

The Egyptians built their pyramids so well that after almost 5000 years they still stand.

Pre-historic Civilizations

Recent excavations cast surprising light on civilizations of the past. Baghdad Museum has lately placed on exhibition an electric engine indicated to be 4500 years old. And it still works, said a Belgian magazine.

Some astronomical instruments brought up from the sea by Greek fishermen, and now on exhibition in a museum in Athens, far supersede today's science. Maybe these are some of the instruments Constantine had thrown into the sea when he began the work of plunging the Roman Empire into darkness that lasted a thousand years in order to crush out ancient religious systems to clear the path for his new one that came to be called Christianity.

A Russian magazine tells of ruins of the Temple of Baalbek (Lebanon), with 2000-ton stone blocks — no apparent way they could have been lifted into place. Also radioactive beryllium found there. Scientists add it up as "earlier visitations from Space People."

An esoteric source claims that 243 feet below the Great Pyramid is a room containing a giant generator which is still function able.

TRUTH IS STRANGER THAN FICTION. Many strange things happen but nothing is too strange to happen.

Of every tree of the garden thou mayest freely eat; but of the tree of the Knowledge of Good and Evil, thou shalt not eat; for in the day thou eatest thereof thou shalt surely die *(Genesis 1:16, 17)*.

"Consider this also, Oh son, That God hath freely bestowed upon man, above all other living things, these two, to wit, Mind and Speech or Reason, Equal to immortality." *(HERMES TRISMEGISTUS)*

"Honest investigation and criticism lead to light and liberty, whereas all forms of suppression lead to darkness and enslavement." *(LIFT THE VEIL)*

You think the DARK AGES are gone because you are asleep. AWAKE!!! Your boasted liberty and enlightenment are largely imaginary. You cannot miss what you never had.

GOLDEN AGE

THE PEOPLE THAT SIT IN DARKNESS SHALL SEE A GREAT LIGHT

ANCIENT SECRET WISDOM

Introduction
Gods of the Ancients

In 1904 E. A. Wallis Budge, M.A., Litt.D., "Keeper of the Egyptian and Assyrian Antiquities in the British Museum," wrote this monumental work of two volumes, entitled "*The Gods of the Egyptians*."

Being a Christian, and believing literally the fables and false stories he had been taught concerning the darkness in which the ancient people lived in reference to God, Budge never dreamed that he was writing only the historical adaptation of a spiritual allegory when he related the Egyptian account of the Great God known as As-Ar, Us-Ra, Us-Ari, Ausares, Osiris, and by other names. He believed that this Great God had been a living king in the flesh, and after death was deified by the Egyptians. He mistook fabalism for factualism and attempted to literalize the Egyptian allegories.

The Christian World has never been truthfully taught that the gods of the Ancient Masters were but symbols of Nature and of cosmic agencies, powers and processes. The symbols were employed to mislead the profane and to make more effective and comprehensive the instruction of the elect concerning the mysteries of Life and Cosmic Spirit.

The scientific religion of the Masters (1) taught that the human body is the Temple in which the Cosmic Spirit dwells on the earth place, and instructed man how to care for his body while it was animated by the Holy Spirit, and also (2) revealed the mystery of the Future Life when the body ceases its function and dissolves into dust.

Chapter 1
The Bible

The Bible is the secret scriptures of the Ancient Masters, and is a sealed book. Its esoteric meaning is unknown today except to students of Occultism. Sixteen hundred years of theological study has served only to conceal more securely the secrets of its fables, parables and allegories. This failure results from the refusal of the church authorities to reject the Bible as history and accept it for what it really is.

The Bible is not a book, but a library of books — 9 of them in the Old Testament and 26 in the New. It is not the work of one man nor a group of men, but the accumulated wisdom of a veritable tide of spiritual interest and research, in which work millions of men have been involved.

Such parts of the Bible as deal with Man, Life and Spirituality, are the literary extensions and amplifications of the symbology of the Zodiac.

In the starry skies the Masters discovered the story of Creation. They knew that creative history had been enacted on a Cosmic scale in the heavens before it was repeated and copied in the human drama on the earth.

The heavenly man, in whose image the earthly man is made, and in whose body the suns and planets are but cells and organs, is the prototype of man himself. Knowing this, the Masters taught their disciples to build life after the pattern of things in heaven. The planisphere was the graph of the Cosmic Man.

Chapter 2
Astral Influence

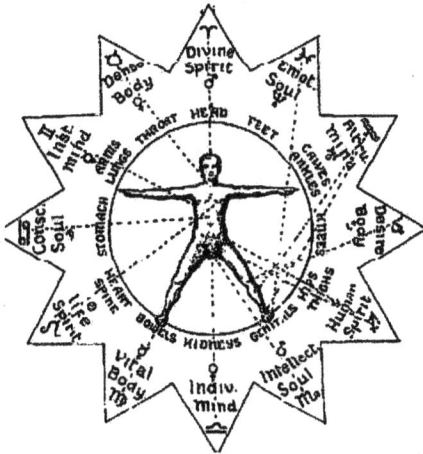

The scientific religion of the Masters formed one system. It was developed thru long ages of time and intensive study of the forces of the Universe. They were Naturists in the fullest sense of the word.

From their Study, the Masters evolved the Zodiac as their Grand Symbol to embody and also conceal their discoveries, and used it as a chart to teach their disciples and followers the mysterious lessons of Life.

We of today have little correct knowledge of what the Zodiac actually means. But we have learned enough to know that it symbolizes the Universe, both visible and invisible; and that in this symbol is contained and concealed the discoveries of the Masters concerning the mysteries of the processes of Creation.

In long ages of work, the Masters discovered the influence of the Astral Bodies of the Universe upon the earth and its people. About all we know now in general of these Cosmic forces is, that the moon rules the tides of the seven seas.

Consider further evidence of planetary influence: The Earth emerged from Pisces, the Water Sign, about 1881 AD, which it entered about 276 B.C. For 2,157 years, the Earth and its people were under the Cosmic influence of that Sign. Witness the inventions of that period having relation to water — the canoe; the ships of the seas, the water wheel, water power, steam engine, irrigation, etc.

About 1881 A.D. the Earth entered Aquarius, the Air Sign; and already under its influence we behold how human inventions have changed. They are now concerned with the air -- wireless telegraphy, air-ships, rocket planes, atomic bombs, radio, radar, atomic energy, and we are only entering the Air Age.

About 50,000 years ago, the Earth entered this same Air Sign. During its reign of 2,157 years there occurred the air and atomic inventions of that era, but the records of these are largely lost and destroyed.

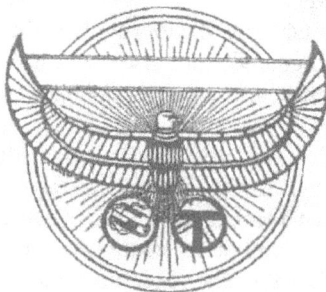

The evidence uncovered by archeologists in the last half century discloses some remarkable things. It shows that man had then developed airships, cosmic ray guns, and giant machinery, powered by atomic force, that quarried rocks out of the hills, formed stone temples out of solid rock, built huge pyramids of stone, many of which still stand to the amazement of the modern world the engineers of this age admit they don't know how the work was done and that we have no machinery that could do it.

The Earth circles our Sun every 365.24 days; and our Sun circles its great Sun, Alcyon, every 25,880 years. The Earth travels around our Sun at the rate of 1080 miles per minute, and turns on its axis at the rate of 1040 miles per hour. A rifle bullet travels 33 miles per minute.

All these function of the Universe have been going on for billions of years, and may never have had a beginning. How could they start? Who or what could start them? And what was the state of things before they started?

Man has been on earth for millions of years, and has always existed potentially. He has seen this old world make these grand cycles many times, and has studied the effects and recorded the results. He concealed his discoveries and secrets from the profane in the Signs of the Zodiac and in the allegories of the Bible. In our stupidity we read these ancient scriptures literally, and get from them little but false suggestions and misleading impressions, exactly as was intended by the Masters who wrote them.

We read of Ezekiel's wheels; the "book with seven seals;" "the Great Red Dragon" that stood before the woman, to devour her child as soon as it was born *(Revelation 5:12)*.

Not a preacher in Christendom can correctly interpret these parables. For they know nothing about the Seven Etheric Centers in the body thru which the Etheric Energy functions, and of which the "book" is a symbol. They never suspect that the Great Red Dragon is a symbol of carnal lust in the blood.

Consider the country of Yucatan, just across the channel from Cuba. It is filled with the remains of ancient civilizations, with inscriptions on stone monuments extending back more than 200,000 years.

When the Christian missionaries of Europe saw the ruins of these ancient structures, they turned green with envy to behold that their religion had been anticipated by the "ancient heathens;" and they falsely wrote that the structures were built about 1500 years ago, and that in some unexplainable way European Christianity had reached these "heathens." That is a typical illustration of how our historic and encyclopedic accounts of the ancient world have been falsified to support a false religion and mislead the multitude. For the church teaches that before the birth of Christianity, mankind was only a savage who worshipped idols, wooden images, etc.

The Catholic bishop Landa, who accompanied the Spanish soldiers under Cortez in the 16th Century, promptly got in his Christian work of destroying the evidence of the grandeur of the ancient civilizations in Yucatan. He ordered the burning of thousands of books and many large manuscripts of parchment, found in the ruins of these ancient temples. These works contained the Cosmic Science of the Ancient Masters handed down from the days of Adam. He also destroyed over 5,000 statues and some 200 vases.

Cogolludo, in his "Historia de Yucatan," wrote: "The (Christian) Spanish chronicles do not give one reliable word about the manners, customs and religion of the builders of the grand edifices that were the objects of admiration to them, as they are now to modern travelers" (Book 4, page 177).

That is an example of the manner in which the histories and encyclopedias possessed by the Christian world have been compiled, falsified, and distorted. The accounts of the ancient world contained in these works have been prepared by Christians and censored by church authorities, in order to protect Christianity from being exposed for what it is. Nowhere in the pages of history can one find a greater fraud.

True accounts of the ancient world are now being dug from the ruins of the past by the archeologists; but even these accounts are falsified and distorted before they are allowed to reach the multitude in printed form.

Chapter 3
Age of Man

The average man never suspects that our histories and encyclopedias have been written by Orthodox Christians who are always striving to conceal the past and support their religious theories. There is in general circulation no true history of the ancient world and the religion of its people. According to what history we have, civilization is a gradual evolution through ages in all parts of the world, "from that intermediate condition between ape-hood and manhood, which we know must have existed, but of which no positively demonstrable evidence has ever been discovered!" {Americana Ency. 1938, volume 2, page 152).

Since it is admitted that there is "no positively demonstrable evidence" that the condition described ever existed, then we must assure that it did exist, or reject the very suggestion that it ever existed.

As we trace back, searching for evidence of the "apehood" days of man, the fine arts of the ancient world burst upon us at once in the glory of their highest perfection.

For instance, the fine arts never attain perfection at once. At all times and in all countries they have passed through a series of crude attempts and imperfect beginnings before they reach perfection. But as the archeologist digs into the ruins of ancient Egypt, evidence of the fine arts burst upon him at once in the grandeur of amazing perfection.

Science now holds that the Earth is billions of years old. Doctor W. C. Pei, research fellow of the Chinese National Geological Survey that uncovered the "Peking man's remains near Peiping in 1929," said, according to the press of July 30,

1948, that "there was a dawning of human life in China fifty million years ago — the Peking man proves it."

In a certain valley in the Himalayas, carved out of solid rock by the use of atomic energy, there are vast caverns in which are deposited and carefully guarded all ancient script covering the history of Man from the dawn of the race, with maps of the ancient world in the days of Lemuria and Atlantis.

These scriptures are not the stories of men, women, kings, queens, cities, geographical, historical, etc. None of them are dated, as that would serve no useful purpose. For these writings are in the form of fables, parables, allegories and symbols, dealing not with gods and saviors, not with systems of religion and forms of superstition, but with the psychological,   physiological,   anatomical, chemical, and astrological aspects   of   the   Hunan   Organism   and its Animating Principle.

The subjects of these scriptures are Man's creation, his fall (physical birth) his salvation (spiritual birth), and his future life.

Researchers for hundreds of years into the distant past all agree,   that   thousands   of   ancient   writings,   tablets, carvings, show that the Ancient Scientists, over a period of ages upon ages, prepared for the elect and left as secret doctrine; amazing records of the human organism, its creation, and its destiny.

To conceal the Ancient Wisdom from those not entitled to receive the same, the records were skillfully prepared in the form of fables, parables, allegories, symbols, susceptible to various meanings, and confusing to those without the Key to the Secret Doctrine.

The Ancient Wisdom Teaches what man should know in order to live the perfect life. Fundamentally they teach Cosmic Science:

1. The Law of Birth
2. The Law of Death
3. The Law of Degeneration
4. The Law of Regeneration
5. The Law of Immortality

Chapter 4
Modern Fallacies

Physical science declares that light travels from the Sun to the Earth in eight minutes, a distance of some 92 million miles. To question, that theory a few years ago meant ostracism from the circle of the elect who knew things.

Late discoveries of the Chemist, as he goes back and begins to tread the soil where stood the ancient alchemist ages ago, show that light and heat are simply rates of motion of a substance that does not travel from star to star, nor from sun to planet, but vibrates in its place at rates in harmony with Universal Energy. This substance, aerial or etheric, travels not, but is everywhere present — the substance of Omnipresent Being.

Another modern theory exploded is that relating to "disease.' It is not known that so-called disease is only an imaginary entity that does not exist. That is the explanation why a thousand years of medical research for "cures of disease" have left the medical profession empty handed — with not one "cure" for any so-called disease. There are two conditions that appear in the body: (1) Good Health and (2) Bad Health. There is no disease. It is the symptoms of Bad Health that doctors are trained to study, group together, and give them names which mean nothing.

This fraud is termed medical art. It is supported by centuries of fraudulent teaching by which the doctors, who live and thrive on the miseries of man, have created a false psychology that yields gigantic profits; and woe unto him who interferes with that profitable racket by teaching Truth.

Chapter 5
Temple of Man

FIGURE 10

Figure ten is a photographic reproduction after Clavigero. It presents the names of the years in the

eclipse period.

There is but one Temple in the world, and that is the body of Man. Nothing is holier than that high from. Man is the miracle of miracles — the great inscrutable Mystery Carlyle.

Due to the false teaching of his cunning leaders, man ignorance and delusion appear in man thing he does. But in none are these qualities more apparent than in matters of Health and Religion.

By deceptive teaching, man is led to believe that Health and Religion are so foreign to each other, that they are not even related, and should never be mixed and crossed in any discussion. That theory is typical of the ignorance of the average individual of the biblical teachings.

The Bible does not support that theory. It says: "Know ye not that ye are the Temple of God, and that the Spirit of God dwelleth in you? If any man defile the Temple of God, him shall God destroy; for the Temple of God is holy, which Temple ye are." (*I Corinthians 3:16, 17*).

"Know ye not that your body is the Temple of the Holy Ghost which is in you, and which ye have of God, and ye (your body) are not your own; for ye are bought with a price; therefore, glorify God in your body, and in your spirit, which are God's" (*I Corinthians 6:19, 20*).

The Bible definitely directs man to glorify himself in his body, hence religious teaching should instruct man how to care for his body, that it may be a fit Temple in which to glorify himself.

A foul body, reeking in filth, is a poor place in which to glorify even a beast. Correct health teaching shows man how to purge and purify his body, that he may obey the biblical command, and in his body glorify himself.

That is the teaching of the Ancient Masters who wrote the scriptures from which the Bible was compiled. The care of the body had a high place in their theology. They studied man and treated him as a Unit — What was good for his body was good for his soul, and vice versa.

Man

The motto of the Ancient Masters was: "Man, know thyself and thou wilt know the Universe and the Gods." That motto was inscribed on the Temple of Delphi.

Due to the destruction of the ancient philosophy and the Ancient Masters in the 4th Century, and the subsequent battle between spiritualism and materialism that grew out of the dark ages produced by that destruction, man has grown so ignorant as to his God, his body, and its animating force, that Alexis Carrel, one of the great medical wen of modern times, wrote a book in 1935, which he titled "*Man, The Unknown*," because so little is actually known now of man and the physiology of his organism.

In that work Carrel made this frank admission: "The science of man is still too rudimentary to be useful. — In fact, our ignorance (of man) is profound." That is quite different from the medical propaganda that appears in the public press.

The reason carrel gives for his ignorance of man is the conquest of the material world, which has ceaselessly absorbed the attention and will of man, caused the organic and the spiritual world to fall into almost complete oblivion.

Figure 6 is a calendar wheel of the Duran type it presents the names of the four seasons and distribution of days in seasons.

Carrel's statement is wrong. The spiritual world fell into almost complete oblivion because modern science proclaims that it is an exhibition of rank superstition for anyone to have faith in such a fantastic realm.

Carrel continues: "The study of spiritual life and of philosophy attracted greater men than the study of medicine. The laws of mysticity became known before those of physiology."

A frank admission by a great scientist that the Ancient Masters who turned to the study of spirituality and philosophy, were "greater men" than the common run of those men lured into the fold of that base fraud termed "medicine." The prejudiced Carrel is wrong again when he asserts that the laws of mysticity became known to the Masters before those of physiology. Even to this day medical art has no Law of Psychology, and blindly asserts that "all is physical matter and mechanical energy."

So-called modern medicine came out of the Dark Ages, and can no more shake off its old superstitions than a man can change the color of his hair. For to do so would utterly destroy medical art.

As the Roman Empire declined with the birth and development of Christianity, the church rapidly assumed more authority, revelation replaced reason; the cause of human ailments became the possessions by demons, and relief was attempted by exorcism or miracles. The four gospels are shot thru and thru with this illogical doctrine. Modern medicine has simply replaced the demons with germs. That's the only difference.

As the power of the church increased, rational thinking was practically forbidden and replaced by superstition. The teachings of able men were cast aside and replaced by ridiculous theories and methods, which originated in fanaticism and grew upon the ignorance of the people.

It was the uncanny knowledge of the Masters concerning the Law of Physiology that led to their discovery of the laws of mysticity. Their knowledge enabled them to understand these laws. It enabled them to realize that the body is literally the Temple of Man, being only a material instrument thru which the Cosmic Spirit contacts the earth plane. They knew that Cosmic Spirit is limited in its manifestations on the visible plane by the kind of body in which it incarnates, and the condition of that body. This Ancient Wisdom revealed the secret that Man is really Cosmic Spirit, dwelling in a material temple, and that man, therefore, has Eternal Life. If such knowledge should ever become the property of the people in general, it would mean the end of the church.

The Masters taught that "it is the spirit that quickeneth (the body); the flesh profiteth nothing" (*John 6:63*). The flesh is material, remains material, and dissolves as material in physical death. The Bible says so (*Ecclesiastics 12:7*).

The Masters knew so much about the Science of Man, that they even listed the four kingdoms of flesh on which man's existence rests at its corners — man, beast, bird and fish — the four quarters of the ancient Zodiac (I Corinthians 15:39). But since the 4th Century these wise Masters have been scorned as pagans and heathens; and during the Dark Ages Christian Europe was taught that this Ancient Wisdom was pure sorcery.

It is unknown now that the Masters prepared the Zodiac as a secret, scientific scripture, dealing with the requirements of men, races and nations. They devised the pictures that mark the constellations, and knew the natural divisions and physiology of the human body. They understood the origin of the spirit monads and comprehended the Cycle of Involution of God to Man, and of Evolution of Man to God. They realized how the fate of Man would ebb and flow between Light and Darkness, between cultureless and barbarism. They discovered this secret in the stars, and pictured it in the signs of the Zodiac and their paranatellons. Astronomy thru its astrological expressions was their Golden Key. It constituted the written law.

In the tomb of Ramses, who reigned 3500 years ago, there was found a massive circle of wrought gold, divided into 365 degrees, and each division marked the rising and setting of the stars for each day. According to Champollion, the tomb of Ramses V at Thebes contained tables of the constellations and of their influence on man for every hour of every month of the year.

The Egyptian Masters taught that a mutual dependence exists between all things in the Universe, ruled by one law, including a mysterious relation between the Spirits of the Stars and the Souls of men. The destiny of mortals was regulated by the motions of the heavenly bodies, just as the moon rules the ebb and flow of the tides. From the conjunction of the planets at the hour of birth, they prophesied what would be the temperament of an infant, what life it would likely live, and what death it would die.

These Masters, ten thousand years ago, knew the shape and movement of the Earth, and how to calculate solar and lunar eclipses. They foretold with remarkable accuracy what was about to happen to mankind, the failure or abundance of crops; and by means of their long continued observation, they foresaw earthquakes, deluges, rising of comets, and all those phenomena, the knowledge of which appears impossible to common comprehension. Yet modern scientists attempt to discredit the wisdom of these Masters by asserting they knew nothing of the laws of physiology.

Then something happened. All this mighty wisdom came to an abrupt end in the 4th Century, when the Cosmic Science, philosophy and temples of the Masters were ruthlessly destroyed, and a new order of darkness was born. Out of that long, dark night which followed as a result of the destruction of the Ancient Wisdom, there came the fatal theories of super naturalism, materialism, and evolution. These fatal theories rule the western world today.

In religious matters, the theological doctrine of super naturalism directly antagonizes physical science, which very properly declares, 'There is no supernatural."

The term "supernatural," and the preposterous propositions involved, drive a purely rational mind to the other extreme. It is this dogma that goads the scientific skeptic into characterizing as mere superstition the loftiest perceptions of the Soul. The atheist, materialist and evolutionist are the product of theological dogma.

With the invention of the theories of materialism — and evolution, there came a need for literature to discredit the ancient doctrine of the soul. In 1922 one of these evolutionists, Paul Lafargue, wrote a book in which he scornfully said:

"The soul, the immaterial life principle, which abandons the body after death to continue its existence in heaven or hell, is an invention of savages that has been perfected by civilization."

The scientific theory of materialism now stands discredited before the world. Physical science has discovered that the base of all Matter is Spiritual. And thus the theory of materialism of the evolutionists of the 19th Century is thoroughly exploded. The atomic theory of matter, which held the field of science for more than a century, has vastly changed thru the discovery of radium.

The atom is no longer the ultimate. It can be resolved into hundreds of electrons The evolutionist can no longer successfully deny the existence of the Spiritual World of the ancient "savages." We may not be able to conceive what it resembles. It may wholly baffle our imagination. But in the name of science we cannot logically dispute its reality. Everywhere the Bible represents that world as being so close to us that, in physical death, the soul enters it "in the twinkling of an eye" (*I Corinthians 15:52*).

Today, by the aid of astronomy, psychology, psychoanalysis, physiology, comparative religion, comparative mythology, and all the other branches of learning that concern "man's relation to the Universe," we are finding the road that leads on to the profound mysteries of Ancient Science. We are discovering that Matter is condensed Spiritual Substance, and that the body is literally the Temple of Man. Hence, it is our primary duty to learn how to keep our body healthy and vigorous, that it may be a fit Temple in which to deify Man.

Chapter 6
Natural Science

The word Nature comes from "nasce," to be born. It means the existing order of things; all of creation; the material world. The definition may be extended to include the spiritual world.

Nature is that which really is. True science is a correct description of how it is while logical reasoning is the process of the description. The Ancient Masters were students of Nature. They were Naturists of the first order. Their system of worship was Naturism. Their gods symbolized the Powers of Nature. The supreme ruler of it all was the Cosmic Power of the Universe.

In their study of the destiny of man, the Masters logically turned to Nature for guidance. In her vicissitudes in the vegetable kingdom, Nature seemed to pass thru a process of dissolution and revival.

The Universal Power was identified with the changes in Nature; and the forces in Nature symbolized in the religious dramas of the Ancient Mysteries was worshipped with imitative and sympathetic rites.

The Ancient Masters concentrated on those eternal attributes of these forces before which men in all ages, when guided by the true light, have instinctively bowed down, and before which even our ablest scientists are constrained to bend in awe and reverence, if not in adoration. To term these Ancient Masters heathens and idolaters is not only gross injustice to them and their work, but an admission of modern ignorance.

These Masters reasoned that we may discover the qualities and powers of Creation by studying its work. No better object was offered for this study than man himself. As man is produced by the same powers that produce all natural phenomena, he must be subject to all its laws. So by studying the processes of Creative Forces in Nature, the Masters determined both the origin and destiny of Man.

Of the Creative Power, that most ancient Egyptian Book of the Dead said "I have the power to be born a second time (*John 3:3, 5, 7*). As Spirit, I enter the body as man and come forth again as Spirit, and look down upon my form which is that of man."

To the Neophyte the great Hierophant of the Ancient Mysteries said "Cast your eyes upon this motionless figures. After death, you yourself will resemble it."

In the ancient scriptures there is only one story. The Masters who did the writing had but one narrative to relate. The series of allegories in the Christian Bible do not cover a wide range of conditions, but the same condition in endless repetition. That central theme is the (1) Incarnation of Spirit in Matter, and (2) Life Eternal. The whole work is summed up in this statement: "The words that I speak unto you, they are spirit, and they are Life" (*John 6:63*).

When Cosmic Spirit becomes incarnate to produce Man, it was implied that, in analogy to his assured Character, he knew all the conditions of his visible existence. This Ancient Wisdom passed down thru the Masters until the days of the 4th Century A.D., when a newly-born theology destroyed the Ancient Wisdom by literalizing the biblical allegories and thus making things appear in a false light.

The deep secrets of Cosmic Processes discovered by the Masters, were concealed from the world at large by fables, parables, allegories, fiction and symbols. They never dreamed that supposedly intelligent men would at a later day become so depraved and ignorant as to interpret these literally.

The Masters always wrote under the forms of figure, without suspecting that the wisest savants of a distant era would be so blinded by the forces of obscurantism as not to realize that the ancient writings spoke only in terms of those earthly forms that adumbrate spiritual realities.

As man is an epitome of the Universe, he is subject to its laws. So the Masters were on solid ground when they cited vegetation as a graphic example of Cosmic Processes, and used that principle to teach the Neophyte the processes of Creation. Scientifically applying creative law to man, they drew an augury of human immortality by reference to the planting and sprouting of grain.

Apollonius of Tyana, born February 16, A.D., died at Ephesus in A.D. 103, was the Great Philosopher of the first century. He was a Master of the Ancient Mysteries of Greece, Egypt, and India. He was employed and used by the Roman Emperor Vespasian as his oracle and magician.

Apollonius preached the essence of the Hindu religion at Rome, Athens, Antioch, Philippi, Ephesus, Alexandria, Jerusalem and many other places. He went to Jerusalem when he was 33 years old. On his approach he was hailed with hosannas and songs of praise to one "that cometh in the name of the Lord" (*Matthew 21:9*). He was the Paul of the New Testament, the Jesus of the four gospels, the author of the so-called John gospel and the Revelation. The so-called Pauline Epistles were compiled from his work. All his writings were interpolated and distorted by the compilers of the New Testament.

In *1 Corinthians 15:35* Apollonius explained the Resurrection Doctrine by propounding the questions, How are the dead raised up? and with what body do they come? He then examined the process of Nature by employing as examples certain agricultural analogies, well-known to every farmer. He began with fundamentals by observing the Law of Germination as a prelude to a comprehension of Spiritual, not physical, Resurrection.

Apollonius of Tyana

Greek Christ of the First Century who taught the doctrines of Chrishna to the West as the basis of a new religion, first called Chrishna and later Christianity. This statue of Apollonius represents him when over 100 years of age, before his departure for India, which he reached when 108 years old.

As can be seen, he enjoyed perfect health and possessed a godlike figure. This was due to his strict raw fruitarian diet which he adapted at the age of sixteen and strictly adhered to ever since. Did the early Christians of the Catacombs worship him under the figure of Orpheus?

Man is a child of Nature, and in the realm of Nature, reasoned Apollonius, that which is sown must die to be re-born (*1 Corinthians 15:36*).

That fact is common knowledge. That is the Law of Nature. That is the scientific explanation of the "born again" doctrine of the Masters, which modern theologians do not understand themselves and treat as a deep mystery. When the principle is understood, the "mystery" becomes so simple as to be understood by a child. Truth is simplicity and simplicity is Truth.

However, the words "die" and "death" in the philosophy of the Masters did not imply extinction, as men have been falsely taught since the 4th Century. The Masters used these terns as another name for Renovation, Rebirth. For the Cosmic Power in man is the same as, and no less than, that which constantly renews vitality in all the realms of Nature.

We find the true Light as false theories crumble before the march of Knowledge based on Truth. Recent discoveries that visible matter is solidified spiritual substance have shocked physical science.

We now begin to comprehend the teaching of the Masters -- that the invisible things of Creation are understood by their visible manifestation (*Romans 1:20*), and that Birth and Death are but names applied to the visible manifestation of changes occurring constantly in the Creative Cycle.

We shall quote the words of the Masters whom the modern world calls pagans and heathens: "Those who have attained the wisdom of the Inner Doctrine; know the mysteries of life, and are not moved by aught that cometh to pass in this world of change. To them, such Life and Death are mere words, and both are but the surface aspects of the Invisible Being. The Real Man is neither born, nor doth it die. Unborn, undying, ancient, perpetual and eternal, it has endured and will endure forever. The body may dissolve, but He who hath occupied it remaineth unharmed and unchanged.

"Free thyself from the deluding pairs of opposites, the changeful aspects of finite existence. Be not deceived by the illusion of appearances and false knowledge.

"When thou shalt rise above the visible plane of illusion, then shalt thou cease to care about doctrines, theology, disputations concerning rites or ceremonies, and other useless trimmings upon the cloth of spiritual thought. Then shalt thou be liberated from attachments to sacred books, or writings of learned theologians, who would interpret that which they fail themselves to understand."

SERPENT OF CREATION

Birth And Death

Birth and Death are two deluding aspects of the same thing. Physical birth may be termed spiritual death, and spiritual birth is regarded as physical death. For due to false teaching, man is never more spiritually dead than when physically alive.

The condensation of the spirit builds the body that appears to be born; and the animating spirit that leaves the body and reunites with the Divine Essence, appears to die. These appearances are misleading illusions. We reason from what we THINK we see, and say that man dies, or the Sun rises — whereas man only appears to die, and the Sun only appears to rise.

Birth into the physical world may be termed death as we leave the spiritual world, the Kingdom of Heaven. What we term death in the physical world is actually birth in the spiritual world as we pass on to that glorious Future Life.

Creative processes move in cycles; and the Soul could not be eternal on the one side, and not be on the other. Knowledge based on truth takes the sting out of death. "O grave, where is thy victory?" (*I Corinthians 1:15; 55*)

The Creator is One, the same as One electricity in each of the millions of light globes.

Ye are gods; and all of you are the children of the most High (*Psalm 82:6*). There is One Intelligence, One Substance, One Life, One Spirit, One God. All is One and One is All.

Such was the natural philosophy of the so-called pagans, heathens, and barbarians of fifty thousand years ago.

Chapter 7
No Death

"If a man die, shall he live again?" (*Job 14:14*). That burning question rises with the dawn of the race, and was answered by the Ancient Masters.

By Death in this case is meant the total extinction of man when his physical body ceases its function.

The spiritual intuition of man declares, "There is no death." The Soul of man rejects the theory of annihilation, advanced by modern science. Man universally harbors the hope of a Future Life. the expectancy of Immortality characterizes both the savage and the savant.

As those intuitions of man are universal, they are natural. Natural impulses imply a natural law of fulfillment. A natural desire that is universal portends a natural means of its accomplishment. Universal tendencies are obviously based upon universal principles. Man is not an object foreign to the Universe. He is an integral part of it, and is ruled and affected by universal laws exactly the same as are all other parts of the Universe. He is the product of Cosmic Elements and Cosmic Forces, exactly the same as are all other existing things.

In common phenomena of Nature, in the ebb and flow of the tides, the waxing and waning of the moon, the changes of the seasons, the growth and dissolution of vegetation, the disintegration of the various bodies, the Ancient Masters saw the Law of Cyclicity, and as to Man, they termed it Born Again.

With the seasonal dissolution (death) of plants, and their recurrent rebirth in the spring, they beheld the Resurrection of Nature, a universal in mortality in all living things, including Man, the most exalted creature on earth.

In the regular journey of the planets, the sun, moon and stars, the Ancient Masters discovered the infallible laws of Nature, and the existence of a universal order pervading all things. They applied these laws to man.

For all visible bodies are made of the same universal elements, by the sane universal creative principle, and are subject to the same laws. The elements of which water, grass and trees are made are the same, and spring from the same source as those of which man's body is made. The same Creative Principle performs the work in all instances, in the same way, under the sane law. Then it follows by logic and reason that under the Law — of Cyclicity and the Law of Analogy; Man is as eternal and immortal as all the rest of Nature. In fact, as Matter is eternal and indestructible, Life could not be less.

It was from this lawful, logical, scientific reasoning that came forth the Secret Doctrine. Except a man be born again, he cannot enter into the Kingdom of Heaven (*John 3:3, 5, 7*).

For more than a millennium thousands of preachers have tried to explain that passage. But they cannot explain that which they fail themselves to understand.

Science has shown that all natural phenomena move in cycles. Nothing has either beginning or ending. Matter is eternal and indestructible. So is Life.

The Creative Cycle moves from the invisible to the visible, and vice versa. A common example of this process is water. As invisible vapor it floats in the air. When cold lowers its vibratory rate, it condenses and becomes visible as water, a compound of invisible gases. A still lower temperature transforms water into ice.

Raising the temperature reverses the process. The ice becomes water and then vapor, and returns to the invisible realm, called the kingdom of Heaven.

That creative cycle is universal and common to all things. But it becomes more complex in understanding and explanation as we advance in the scale of natural phenomena.

Passing from water, the simple form, to man, the most complex, we find the same creative process in operation. But the explanation is more complicated. In their search for the secret of the Future Life thousands of years ago, it was analyzed and solved then by the Ancient Masters.

When invisible vapor becomes visible as water, that is Birth into the visible realm. When water CHANGES to invisible vapor and returns to the invisible (spiritual) realm, it is BORN AGAIN and enters into the kingdom of Heaven.

That is the secret "change" to which the Masters referred. "If a man die, shall he live again?' All the days of my appointed time will I wait, till my CHANCE come" (*Job 14:14*).

THERE IS NO DEATH! "We shall not sleep (in death), BUT WE SHALL ALL BE CHANGED" (to Immortality), said the Masters (I Corinthians 15:51). And so, 'Death is swallowed up in victory. O death; where is thy sitting? O grave, where is thy victory? (*1 Corinthians 15:54, 55*) Then the scheming priest who helped to compile the New Testament, added this illogical passage: The sting of death is sin; and the strength of sin is the law" (*1 Corinthians 15:56*). Those empty words mean nothing.

The Masters explained that when the Celestial Body enters the terrestrial body called Man, he is Born into the visible realm of the kingdom of Heaven. Of that event we think nothing unusual because it is so cannon and so well understood.

But the deceived and misled multitude little knows that when man's terrestrial body dissolves (dies) and the Spirit leaves that physical envelope, Man is in truth BORN AGAIN, to begin a new existence, and he enters into that vast invisible realm, termed the kingdom of Heaven, a mere figure of speech, invented for the purpose of deception.

For as the whole Universe, both the visible and invisible realms, are in fact the kingdom of Heaven, man is never out of it, even tho he may so think in his ignorance. That mysterious "change" from the visible to the invisible state (in the twinkling of an eye), was well explained by that great Hierophant, Apollonius, called Paul in the Bible. Yet the simplicity of the truth of his teachings has been destroyed by the distorted manner in which the "blind leaders of the blind" have handled it. The religious philosophy of the Masters was based on that Natural Science of the Universe which includes both the visible (physical) and invisible (spiritual) worlds. They considered man as a dual being, composed of spiritual force and physical substance (*I Corinthians 15:44*). Their philosophy was founded upon all the facts in all the departments of Nature, omitting none.

The facts of Nature and the principles of Truth are changeless. But the flimsy theories of modern scientists change with the seasons. What they proclaim as Truth today they reject tomorrow as error. The eternal Truth of the Immortality of Man remains changeless throughout the centuries. It was a matter of common knowledge with the Ancient Masters, who are now termed pagans and heathens by the modern world. The best way to discredit Ancient Wisdom is to degrade its developers. The certainty of apparent physical death is patent to all. But few there be today who know the mysterious secret of exactly what happens when that dreaded event occurs. dreaded only because of the ignorance and false teaching surrounding it.

In the Ancient Mysteries the Neophyte was taught the carefully guarded secret that there is no dying, no death, no extinction of the Real Man. There is only a transition, a change: "In the twinkling of an eye we shall all be changed." And thus is destroyed the last enemy termed death (*1 Corinthians* 15:26), which has no existence except in the mind.

The words die and death were used symbolically in the Mysteries to describe the descent of the Spirit into physical substance, and so the body was allegorically the sepulcher of the Soul.

The Masters said, in a spiritual sense, the Soul "dies" or "sleeps" upon entering the body in incarnation. During its days in the physical temple (*1 Corinthians 3:16*), the Soul was considered as sleeping (dead) in the body. This was termed "falling asleep in Hades." The Masters said, "The Soul is now dwelling in the grave which we call the body. ... It is dead so far as it is possible for the Soul to die."

This is the esoteric interpretation of that allegoric imagery, the confusion of which, with the fact of bodily demise, has been a puzzle to the modern world since the destruction of the Ancient Wisdom in the 4th Century A.D. Men are led astray by imputing to words erroneous meanings.

We sow not the body that shall be, said Apollonius (Paul). We sow bare grain (*1 Corinthians 15:37*).

The creative process gives it a body; and to each kind of seed, a body of its own. While the life of the seed, born again in the new plant, may be fabled to die, that is only symbolic. As none could be more logical, so none could be more superficial. The seed dies not in terms of extinction. It simply CHANGES, as Apollonius said.

This Master then elucidates the ancient allegory by differentiating the bodies as celestial and terrestrial. The latter (grain) is sown in corruption; out of which the celestial (spiritual-new life) is raised in incorruption (42). It is sown in dishonor; it is raised in glory; it is sown in weakness; it is raised in power (43); it is sown a natural (physical) body; it is raised a spiritual body. There is a natural body and a spiritual body (44). How could the subject be more clearly explained?

The first man is made a living soul (in the flesh — *Genesis 2:7*). The second man is a spirit (imprisoned in the body of flesh -- 54). The first man (body) is of the earth, earthy; and the second is the spirit (47).

Be sure to grasp this statement of the great Hierophant: "As we (all) have borne the image of the earthy, we (all) shall also bear the image of the heavenly" (spiritual — 1 Corinthians 15:49).

Apollonius (Paul) was a Master of the Mysteries of Greece, Egypt and India. He was the greatest philosopher of his day, and knew many secrets of Nature unknown to the world now. But under his bend of secrecy, he dared not tell all he knew about the Born Again doctrine taught in the Mysteries.

To exemplify the doctrine of Immortality, and to denote the "Only Begotten Son" (*John 1:14, 18 - 3:16, 18),* five thousand years before the Christian era, the Egyptian Mysteries delineated a Scarabaeus (beetle), because this animal is self-begotten, being unconcealed by a female.

The Sacred Beetle also symbolized generation and a father, because it is engendered solely by the father, making the offspring the only begotten son. Massey writes: "Khoper, the beetle, buried himself, with his seed, in the earth; there he transformed, and the father was REBORN as the only begotten son."

This information reveals the source and secret of the "only begotten son of God," mentioned only in the John gospel, of which Apollonius (Paul) was the original author. We read:

"No man bath seen God at any time: The only begotten Son, which is in the bosom of the Father, he hath declared him" (*John 1:18*).

Another Christian fraud uncovered and exposed. Mystery and confusion vanish as the facts are disclosed. When we know the source of this statement, and to what it refers, we not only understand its correct meaning, but find that it is literally true — except that the object involved is a BUG and not a man.

The living beetle, as the father with the son in his bosom, goes under ground, buries himself, to be BORN AGAIN — to issue forth renewed.

The Egyptian Masters employed this phenomenon of Nature to teach the Neophyte more effectively the mystery of the Father or Spirit, incarnating in Matter, and being BORN AGAIN on the opposite horizon as his transformed son. As this natural phenomenon occurs in the case of insignificant insects, it could not be less in the case of man. For it is not logical nor reasonable to believe that God would grant eternal life to bugs and not confer this blessing upon man, the lord of the visible world.

To the Ancient Masters the deepest mystery was the grand cycle of phenomena — birth, life, death or decomposition, and New Life out of death or decay. They discovered the secret of Immortality by studying the creatures that God hath made; and to them the transformation of the worm was a greater wonder than the stars, for it revealed the mystery of Immortality.

Hence, the lowly scarabaeus or beetle was sacred to them as a creature whose conduct revealed and proved the Born Again doctrine of their science and religion.

Thus their remarkable discoveries and faiths are condensed into allegories which they understood, but were not always able to explain in language; for there are thoughts and ideas which no language ever spoken by man has words to express.

Chapter 8
The Resurrection

The votaries of Christianity claim that it is a religious system based on the Bible. The Bible shows that such claim is false. "I believe in . . . the resurrection of the body," is the fraud that everyone must swallow to embrace the Christian faith.

Christianity consists of an (1) unfounded belief in a vicarious atonement, (2) stemming from the alleged crucifixion of a mythical god (*Matthew 27:35*), (3) who strangely and unnaturally rose from the dead (*Matthew 28:7*), and (4) miraculously "washed us from our sins in his own blood." (*Revelation 1:5*).

Such wild, fraudulent claims are contrary to all common sense and reason, and to all the known laws of the Universe. They are disputed, discredited and denied by the biblical text.

Such is the garbled, mutilated and inconsistent story that could be foisted upon the world only by an age of darkness and the surreptitious compilation of the New Testament, which was not born until it was needed in the 4th Century, and then needed only because the Old Testament could not be made to support the fraud.

We must follow cold facts to find the goal of our search. The Bible states that we reap as we sow, (*Galatians 6:7*); and that in death the body dissolves and returns to dust (*Ecclesiastics 12:7*). These natural facts and events harmonize with Universal Law, and have been known and witnessed since the dawn of humanity; and the process is ruled by a law that has no exceptions and changes not. Exceptions belong to the realm of speculation and fiction. It is impossible to conceive that The Unchangeable, in the formulation of His degrees, ever drops a thread or fails to include Universal Existence in one grand plan.

Furthermore, in *1 Corinthians 15:50* the definite statement appears that "flesh and blood" (physical body) "cannot inherit (enter) the kingdom of God (Spiritual Realm); neither doth corruption (the physical) inherit incorruption (the spiritual)." It is also stated that "as we (all) have borne the image of the earthy, we shall (all) also bear the image of the heavenly" (*1 Corinthians 15:49*). This is not conditioned upon any belief. It includes all men, regardless of their belief. It includes all men, regardless of their belief. (*Mark 16:16*).

In spite of these notorious facts, the text of that same chapter the New Testament compilers in the 4th Century twisted and distorted to make it serve their scheme. They devoted verses 12 to 22 of the chapter to a discussion of "the resurrection of the dead," meaning the resurrection of the physical body. Not understanding the esoteric meaning of the biblical terms "resurrection" and "born again," the church, groping in darkness with the multitude, makes a mystery of these simple words.

Reverting to the Ancient Mysteries, it appears that the Neophyte was taught by the Masters that "the Real Man is neither born, nor does he die. Unborn, undying ancient, perpetual and eternal, he has endured and will endure forever. The body dissolves and returns to dust, but He who hath occupied it, remaineth unharmed and unchanged."

It is a fact that if Man comes from the Spiritual World as all religions teach, he must, under the law, return to the source of his origin. That is as obvious and certain as the law of mathematics. Moreover, nothing returns to the Spiritual World because nothing comes out of it. It is not a return but a change in manifestation, as stated by the Masters:

"We shall not all sleep, but we shall all be changed, in a moment, in the twinkling of an eye" (*1 Corinthians 15:51, 52*).

That Hindu philosophy is fifty thousand years old. It was taught to Apollonius (Paul) when he went to India and was initiated into the Mysteries. It was copied from his writings many years after he was dead, when the New Testament was compiled in the 4th Century.

What do these statements mean? How does the change take place? How does man's soul leave the Spirit World, and how does it return? These secrets were taught the Initiates in the Ancient Mysteries.

The Masters held that the Spirit becomes manifest in the body of man when impregnation occurs in the female uterus. That is the condition of its mundane manifestation. That is incarnation. That is the burial of the Soul in Matter. According to the Masters, it is a living death. It is an entombment of the Spirit that carries life on, but under physical conditions, dramatized in the Ancient Mysteries as the "Death of the Soul." That was only a figure of speech.

The Masters said, "The Soul becomes cribbed, cabined and confined" in the limitations of the carnal body, as it loses a dimension of consciousness at each step on the descending image of the earthy, so all men shall also bear the image of the spiritual (*1 Corinthians 15:49*).

Apollonius (Paul) then clearly and definitely rejects the false doctrine of a physical resurrection. For he declares, "now this I say, brethren, that flesh and blood (physical body) cannot inherit (enter) the kingdom of God" (50).

The physical, natural body of man remains subject to the law that rules all physical substance. That body never rises from the grave. It dissolves and returns to dust, just as the Bible says (*Ecclesiastics 12:7*).

"Initiation proper into the Ancient Mysteries," wrote Doctor Angus "was considered a physical death from which the Initiate rose through re-birth (born again). The hour of midnight was often chosen as the most appropriate time for initiation. There was a familiar word-play on the words 'initiation' and 'dying.' 'To die is to he initiated,' said Plato. 'Then to be initiated into the kingdom of God is to die; and death is the supreme initiation.'" And so, in the ceremonies of initiation, the Hierophant pointed to the mummied form of As-ar-us (Osiris), lying on its bier, and to the candidate said: "Cast your eyes upon this motionless figure. After death you will resemble it." The most secret initiation, to which only the most elect were admissible, taught the Neophyte how man's soul leaves the Spirit World and how it returns.

In that most ancient work, The Egyptian Book of the Dead, God is made to say to the candidate, "I have the power to be born a second time (*John 3:3, 5, 7*). As Spirit, I enter the human body, and cone forth again as Spirit, and look down upon my form, which is that called man."

That is incarnation, taught by the Masters as the burial of the Soul in Matter. It is a living death according to the Masters. It is the entombment of the Spirit that carries life on, but under physical conditions, dramatized as Death in the Egyptian Mysteries.

Proclus mentioned an interesting fragment of the ceremonies of the Mysteries relating to the symbolical death and burial in the Dionysiac-Orphic rites, as follows:

"The Hierophant commanded that the body should be buried except the head in the most secret of all initiations, "as a result of which the Spirit in us is Dionysiac (divine) and a veritable image of Dionysus" (*The Mystery Religion*).

The Cross was used in the Mysteries as a symbol of the descent of Spirit into Matter. To represent this, the Neophyte, who had been rendered unconscious by a secret process, was laid upon a fructiform bier, hollowed to fit the body, wearied after a long preliminary ritual. His arms were loosely bound with cords, and he was carried from the Chamber of Initiation into the Crypt, or lower vault of the temple. There he was placed upon a sarcophagus to represent actual burial, and the priests chanted a very ancient dirge over him. He remained here for three days, whilst the tests of earth, water, air and fire were applied to the divorced Soul as a practical experience of its invulnerability.

On the fourth day of the entombment, the Neophyte "was brought forth and exposed to the first rays of the rising Sun, and restored to natural life" by an unknown process. The Superior Masters, knowing much more than we do about the body and its physiology, knew the secret of what to do to the unconscious body to induce the Spirit to re-enter it; and so in the initiation the "dead" was "raised" to life.

Initiation was considered to be a mystical death; a descent into the infernal regions, where every pollution, and the stains and imperfections of a corrupt and evil life were purged away by fire and water; and the perfect Life was then said to be regenerated, reborn, restored to a renovated existence of life, light and purity.

Cicero said that the initiates not only received lessons which made life more agreeable, but drew from the ceremonies happy hopes for the moment of death. Socrates said that those who were admitted to the Mysteries, possessed, when dying, the most glorious hopes for eternity. He added: "The great consummation of all philosophy is Death. He who pursues philosophy alright, is studying how to die" (Pike, page 393). In the finale, initiation was the introduction to the remarkable change of death, mentioned by Apollonius (Paul, *1 Corinthians 15:51*). For death is the true initiation, to which sleep is the introductory or minor mystery.

Death is the final rite that united the Initiate with God. So when the Neophyte was "resurrected," he knew the great secret of initiation. From actual experience he learned the fact that Life is eternal, and did not have to rely on the jargon of some preacher. For as his physical form lay still in physical death, his Spirit hovered over it, and with his spiritual Eyes he saw his unconscious, motionless body.

In his initiation, the Neophyte was shown the figure of Osiris lying on its funeral bier. At the head stood Nephthys, and at the foot, Isis, the two sisters who weep for him. Hovering over the body, symbolical of the Soul, was a "hawk with outstretched wings" (Budge). This was to teach the

Neophyte how the God Spirit looks upon His "form which is that of man."

The story of Lazarus appears to have been unknown to the authors of the synoptic gospels. They never mention it. The account appears only in the fourth gospel, the original of which was written about 67 A.D. by Apollonius (Paul). He was a Master of the Egyptian Mysteries, knew the story, and wrote it as an allegory. It was revised and distorted when literalized by the compilers of the New Testament in the 4th Century.

In the Egyptian Mysteries drama; 5,000 years before the Christian era, Horus symbolically raised his "dead" father, Asar (Osiris) at Anu, by calling unto him in the cave to rise and come forth (John 11:43). When the fable was literalized in the New Testament, Horus became Jesus, Asar became Lazarus, and Anu became Bethany. That easy was it to make these slight changes in the old manuscripts.

The time came when the Hebrews adopted the Egyptian phrases and names, and they changed Asar to El-Asar. Later, the Romans took up the same material and added the Latin "us", making it El-Asar-Us. Then the English took it over, and dropped the E and made it Lazarus. As the ancient records are dug from the ruins, the frauds are exposed.

Also, in the Egyptian drama, the two sisters, Isis and Nephthys were present. An old-source-name for Isis was Meri, basic for the Latin Mare (sea). The Egyptian plural of Meri was Merti. This became Mertae in Latin form. In Hebrew it resolved into what was rendered Martha in English. In the gospel narrative these women, tented Mary and Martha, were called the sisters of Lazarus.

It is amazing to learn how literally the gospel compilers copied from ancient writings. Then they concealed the evidence of their plagiarism by destroying the old manuscripts. But the stone monuments of antiquity were not destroyed, and at last they have yielded up their secrets, and the greatest fraud in history now stands exposed.

In referring to this fable, Massey says: "Asar in Anu, like Lazarus in Bethany, was not dead but sleeping. Horus cones to awaken Asar out of sleep." He continues:

"In one of the earlier funeral texts it is said of the sleeping Asar: 'The Great One waketh, the Great One riseth.' The Manes in Amenta were not regarded as dead, but as sleeping, breathless of body, motionless of heart. Hence, Horus comes to awaken the sleepers in their coffins." Plotinus cites a clear presentment of the ancient Greek conception of the imprisonment of Spirit in Matter:

"When the soul (individualized spirit) had descended into generation, it partook of evil and is carried a great way into a state the opposite of its first purity, to be merged in it, and death to the soul is, while it is baptized or immersed in the material body, to descend into matter and be wholly subjected to it. This is what is meant by falling asleep in Hades."

And here appears the true, basic meaning of the word "baptized." The Ancient Masters taught that to incarnate was to be plunged, baptized, into the watery condition of the body. That is the fundamental definition of baptism in ancient philosophy.

The buried Asar (Osiris) symbolized the Soul buried in Matter, not the body buried in a grave. The grave was the typography used to designate the non-historical burial in the body.

Budge, in his great work, "The Gods of the Egyptians," never suspected that he was writing only the historical adaptation of a spiritual allegory when he said: "But about Osiris' burial-place there is no doubt, for all tradition states that his grave was at Abydos in upper Egypt" (Volume 2, page 146).

Budge believed that Osiris had been a living king, and was later deified. He mistook allegory for realism.

Although it flourished for thousands of years, the civilization of the Pharaohs remained shrouded in mystery until recent times. The true history of the gigantic monuments and the people who built them could not be gleaned from the great accumulation of inscriptions and documents because the art of deciphering their difficult writing was lost.

Then, by chance, in the Nile Delta, near a village called Rosetta, a stone was uncovered on which a lengthy proclamation in hieroglyphics was paralleled in Greek. Here at last was the key scholars needed. The task of piecing together 33 centuries of ancient Egyptian history could begin.

Stobaeus has preserved a fragment of Themistius which says:

"Then the Soul suffers a passion such as that of those who are undergoing initiation into the Greater Mysteries; wherefore also there is a corresponding of word to word and act to act in teleutan teleisthai, teleutan (dying) and teleisthai (initiation), with reference to the Dionysiac or Eleusianian Mysteries."

According to Firmicus Maternus, the intending Mystes of Attis was admitted into the Mysteries as symbolically "about to die."

Due to the terrible oath of secrecy by which they were bound, very little was ever made public by the Initiates of the secret rites and ceremonies of the Mysteries. What little there was published was destroyed by the despots in the 4th Century in order to hide the evidence and make it appear to later generations that prior to that century, and on back to the days of Adam, men were only heathenish idolaters.

The true facts are, that in their Science the Ancient Masters taught the unity of Spirit and the Continuity of Life. According to their philosophy, the immortality of Life is proved in the same way as the indestructibility of Matter. The Masters taught that man lives as a spiritual being; that the Breath of Life energizes his body and makes him a living creature (*Genesis 2:7*); that it is the Spirit which animates the body (*John 6:63*); and that the body is the physical prison of the Soul. In death, the Soul is released from its prison, and returns unto God who gave it (*Ecclesiastics 12:7*).

"The great consummation of all philosophy is death," said Socrates, and he added: "He who pursues philosophy aright, is studying how death releases the Soul from its earthly prison."

This ancient teaching has been lost and destroyed; and today man thinks he is a material being because physical science so declares. The Masters taught that as we lie down in our last sleep, termed death (transition), "we shall all be changed in a moment, in the twinkling of an eye," and we "shall be raised incorruptible" as Spiritual Beings in the Future Life, immortal and eternal (*1 Corinthians 15:50-55*).

For as Matter is both indestructible and eternal, declared the Masters, Life could not be less.

"Ye must be born again. Except a man be born again, he cannot enter the kingdom of heaven" (*John 3:3, 7*).

Transition, termed physical death or physical dissolution, is the mysterious, little understood, but natural process of being "born again," as taught by the Ancient Masters — just as much and certain for man as for grains of wheat and corn. For these are all a part of Nature and subject to the powers of the sane Universal Law.

Chapter 9
Man's Transformation

This chapter is taken from our larger work and included here because of its intimate relation to the subject at hand. It deals directly with the Law of Change (*1 Corinthians 15:50-52*), as enunciated by Apollonius (Paul), and by him taken from Hindu Philosophy.

Since the dawn of humanity, man has witnessed the inexplicable phenomenon of Inert Matter raised up the exalted Life Plane. He has seen the physical form of man emerge from the female creative centers, animated by Solar Force inhaled in the breath of Life (*Genesis 2:7*), and thus observed the Dead raised to Life.

The Masters regarded this as the First Birth.

Then came the return, the Second Birth, from the physical to the spiritual, the born again mystery.

While these things are mentioned in the Bible, they are not understood by the clergy and are erroneously interpreted.

If Spiritual Man is the Real Man, as the Ancient Masters taught, then the Real Man must, under the Law of Change, return unharmed the primary source of his origin, in the Process termed "Born Again" (*Ecclesiastics 12:7; John 3:3, 5, 7*).

This is a natural fact as obvious and certain as the law of gravity or the law of chemical affinity. It is puzzling and obscure only because it is not understood, due to general ignorance and false teaching.

Science has recently shown that the several realms of Nature present the visible appearance of invisible elements in various shapes and forms.

These realms rise successively as invisible elements are transmuted into visible forms. The vitalization of these forms results from the mysterious energy inherent by nature in the universal elements.

When Herodotus (494-425 B.C.) visited Egypt some 450 years before the gospel Jesus was ever thought of, the high priest of the Egyptian Mysteries presented evidence to show that Egyptian history had continued Uninterrupted for 11,340 years (nearly 14,000 years from this date), and informed him that their "Book of the Dead" was by far the most ancient of all holy books.

This work, said to have been written by Thoth, whom the ancient Greeks called Hermes, "Messenger of the gods," taught the existence of a World-Soul, termed the Ba, which produced a World-Body, the Material Universe, and that Man is an epitome of the Universe in which he dwells.

The World-Soul is the Real Man, Eternal Being, whose symbol in the Egyptian Mysteries was a Circle, which represents the Great Cosmic Circuit of Life, flowing from the Sun to Man, and from Man back to the Sun. It was said to be symbolic of "the materialization of Spirit; the manifestation of Spirit in the visible world."

This work taught that man is a dual being, partaking of both the Visible and Invisible Worlds; but modern man knows it not because of false teaching. He is dual in consciousness, but exercises now only the physical aspect because of ignorance and degeneration. He is never more spiritually dead than when physically alive.

In the Egyptian Mysteries the Neophyte was taught that when the physical aspect of man's conscious state is inhibited, or made dormant, or suspended by accident, injury, poison or other causes, he is then in that unconscious state where his Spiritual Consciousness rules, and he experiences the sensation of the Fourth Dimension, wherein Immortality reigns. In the Ancient Masters this faculty was developed and used for their guidance.

This secret is known to Occult Science; but physical science refuses to investigate the matter, claiming it is only a myth of the imagination of the ancient heathens and ape-men. That is what children are taught in the schools and colleges, and the reason why people shun truth because it is so foreign to what they are taught.

The Ancient Masters taught, and correctly so, that there is no death as that word is now commonly understood by the misled masses. There is a state of transition, wherein man's spiritual consciousness rules supreme because it is released from the limitations imposed by the physical organism. Man is then able to see both sides of his dual nature, and to sense his spiritual double as the Real Man, and his physical figure as the shadow man.

At transition (physical death), the substance of the visible body falls entirely out of the range of the great Cosmic Circuit, and, under the law governing inert matter. It returns to the earth as a reservoir (*Ecclesiastics 12:7*). But the subconscious mind (spiritual man) remains intact, unaltered, and unharmed by that mysterious change which appears to occur in the physical man.

In the unconscious state, man's conscious mind is bland and inactive. Suspended are the faculties of seeing (even though the eyes may be open), of hearing, smelling, tasting, and feeling. These five senses of the physical plane are then incompetent to register impressions conveying any intelligence. The conscious mind is closed like a book with seven seals (*Revelation 5*).

The Supreme Universal Consciousness maintains its perpetually active state, so that the physiological processes of the body continue interrupted. In fact, the God Consciousness is so alert that if the unconscious body is removed from a comfortable to a chilly room, the body temperature automatically changes to meet the hostile conditions of the colder environment.

In like manner other disturbances are met. If the arms or legs of the unconscious body are artificially exercised, the physiological processes quicken to supply the additional energy required. That illustrated the Spiritual Consciousness protecting the unconscious body, despite the fact that the unconscious body is not aware of it.

This unconscious state is only temporary. At transition (physical death) a similar condition occurs, but remains permanent. In a word, transition (physical death) is a change of consciousness. The consciousness of the physical body is superseded by the Divine, Universal Consciousness.

In the case of physical death, the Universal Consciousness leaves the body because the body substance has fallen out of the influence of the Great Cosmic Circle of Life. This Divine Consciousness may be termed the Soul, the Immortal Consciousness, withdrawing from the body at the time of transition (physical death).

Medico-science scorns the suggestion of the Spiritual Man and puts all emphasis on the physical man. That part consists largely of fluid, a compound of invisible gases. A man of 150 pounds would weigh 50 pounds if he were thoroughly dried out. The blood is 90 percent water. The bones are nearly half water. The brain is 85 percent water. After cremation of the dead body, a small amount of ash remains that would also dissolve into invisible gas if exposed to greater heat.

That is the end of the visible form which medico-science mistakes for the Real Man. When we blind ourselves by studying the physical side of man only, we can see nothing but his visible form and logically mistake that for the Real Man. In the end we are left empty-handed. For the shadow man is gone.

The Ancient Masters searched farther afield for the Real Man, and found him. They discovered the mysteries of Creation because they studied the other side and found that the visible form is not the Real Man but only the shadow man.

There is one striking feature of the reports of those who have been on the border-line of transition, but did not pass over (*Psalm 104:9*). That is, all these reports agree.

An electrician was shocked by high voltage. He was rushed to a hospital in an unconscious state and not expected to live. The body appeared lifeless, and the undertaker was notified to take it to the morgue. Then the nurses were surprised when they began to feel a little warmth, showing that the man was still alive.

There is the case of a woman, believed to have passed through transition for twenty-four hours. Of a philosopher who was thought to be dead, of a truck driver whose truck was demolished by a train and he lay unconscious for seven days. Of a little girl who was thought to be dead. She was just able to talk and describe in a childish way what she experienced in her unconscious state. She had never heard the things she related, yet her report was identical with all the other. What did they report?

The secret of what occurs in man's mind at the moment of transition and later, was taught in the Egyptian Mysteries. The rites of these religious dramas, "commencing in gloom and sorrow, and ending in light and joy, dimly shadowed forth the strange passage of man from physical mortality to spiritual immortality."

Traces of these things appear in the Bible, but only occult students understand their true meaning: "I will ransom them from the power of the grave" (*Hosea 13:14*). "In the twinkling of an eye, the dead shall be raised incorruptible, and we shall be changed. For this corruptible must put on incorruption, and this mortal must put on immortality." (*1 Corinthians 15:52, 53*)

These dark passages appear in clear light when we know the esoteric weaning. We have only a little knowledge of the ceremonies in the initiations in the Mysteries, and it might all have been lost but for Apuleius (Met., lib. xi), who was initiated in all the several degrees.

He says nothing regarding any of them but the first, the Mysteries of Isis, symbolic of the God of Nature in the Egyptian Mysteries. When he addressed to this Goddess his prayer for initiation, he says she appeared as a beautiful female "over whose divine neck her long, thick hair hung in graceful ringlets." Answering him, she said:

"The parent of Universal Nature attends thy call. The Mistress of the Elements, initiative Germ of Generations, Supreme of Deities, Queen of departed Spirits, first inhabitant of Heaven, and uniform type of all the Gods and Goddesses, propitiated by thy prayers, is with thee. She governs with her nod the luminous heights of the firmament, the salubrious breezes of the oceans; the silent deplorable depths of the shades below; one Sole Divinity under many forms, worshipped by the different nations of the Earth under many titles, and with various religious rites." — Pike.

Directed by the Goddess how to proceed, Apuleius was presented for initiation to the Chief Priest, who addressed him as follows:

"There is not one among the initiated of a mind so depraved, or so bent on his own destruction, as, without receiving a special command from Isis, to dare to undertake her mission rashly and sacrilegiously, and thereby commit an act certain to bring upon himself dreadful injury. For the gates of the shades below, and the care of our life being in the hands of the Goddess (symbolically) — The ceremony of initiation into the Mysteries is, as it were, to suffer death, with the precarious chance of resurrection. Wherefore, the Goddess, in the wisdom of her Divinity, hath the power to select as persons to whom the secrets of her religion can with propriety be entrusted, those who, standing as it were on the utmost limit of the course of life they have completed, may through her Providence be in a manner born again; and commence the career of a new existence" (Pike, page 388).

At this point the language of the Chief Priest is only jargon to the multitude, and only heathenish babble to modern science. But to the occultist, who understand both the symbolical death and resurrection here referred to, it is a profound sermon of great import.

Concerning his initiation, Apuleius was bound by a terrible oath to keep the secret. He says that if he disclosed the secret, it "would affix the penalty of rash curiosity to my tongue as well as to thy ears:" (and if) "I told thee such things that, hearing thou necessarily canst not understand," for the substance of the secret is "beyond the comprehension of the Profane" (Pike).

Then with cautious reticence he says: "I approached the abode of death: with my foot I pressed the threshold of Proserpine's Palace (infernal regions). I was transported through the elements, and conducted back again. At midnight

I saw the bright light of the sun shining. I stood in the presence of the Gods, the Gods of Heaven and of the Shades below; ay, stood near and worshipped" (Pike, page 389).

There Apuleius stops and tells no more. The modern knowledge on this mysterious point of Life comes from those who have been at the border-line of death (transition), as Apuleius was, but did not pass over. Their accounts reveal what the Initiate was taught in the Ancient Mysteries.

The record says that in his initiation, Apuleius suffered a "voluntary death" (ad instars voluntaries mortis) and "approached the realm. of death" in order to thereby attain his "spiritual birthday" (natalem sacrum) in the service of the Goddess, whose followers were "as it were reborn," or Born Again.

Socrates said that participation in the Sacred Mysteries was the greatest of all things, and the source of the greatest blessings. For the happiness there promised is not limited to this mortal life, but extends beyond the grave. There a new life begins, he continued, in which the Initiate enjoys a bliss without alloy and without limit. What is the strange secret that was taught by the Ancient Masters, as revealed by the God Consciousness when the physical body is wavering at the extreme border-line of transition (physical death)?

There is at first a sense of surprising levity of the body. That appears as the first factor which impresses the subconscious mind of the unconscious man, hovering at the very brink of that unknown Spiritual Life, from whence no traveler ever returns when once across that Dark River.

Long before the unconscious man is willing to let nurse or doctor know that strange things are happening, he begins to sense that he is not lying so heavily. At first he thinks it is the imagination. Then he begins to sense pleasant warmth, and to feel that he could rise from the bed and nothing could stop him. The room that was only a few feet distant, begins to appear farther away. It is not due to the fading of his eyesight, as he still recognizes the persons present. It is the secret of the Fourth dimension. He begins to sense himself in a world devoid of both space and time, and to feel that he is existing in the Fourth Dimension. Yet none of the persons mentioned, except the philosopher, had ever heard of that dimension.

Then the voices of those present begin to grow dim, until it seems as if they were at the end of the hall. This is a great moment for the person, because of the fading out of physical impressions.

Eventually, the   unconscious man could see nothing but his physical body lying on the bed. Not with his physical eyes, but with his spiritual sight. Between him and his body appeared a dim haze. The philosopher described it as the aura. Another said it looked like the silver cord mentioned in the Bible (*Ecclesiastics 12:6*). Still another described it as being similar to the umbilical cord, but not so solid. The fact is, they all saw something between them and their body, and they could feel the separation gradually taking place.

Another feature is, they had no desire to return to their physical body to stop the separation; but they did have a feeling of deep sorrow for those weeping around the body. They sense that sorrow and feel they must return to relieve it. But as for themselves, the sense of levity, of great space, freedom from all pain and suffering, the thrill of the new existence, give them an impelling urge to let the change continue and be permanent.

All accounts agree that there seems to be a dual power present — one trying to hold them in the physical body, and the other trying to draw them away; and in that perplexing state some of them waver. Finally, as to those who go through the experience and return, they are drawn back into their physical body. They feel themselves cramped, shut in, and crushed; and immediately their physical sensations begin to return. They begin to feel uncomfortably warm instead of the pleasant cooling sensation. They begin to feel heavy and weighted down, as if there were a weight on their chest. It is difficult to breathe. Their eyelids are hard to open, but they slowly do; that is the first sign they are returning to consciousness. Sometimes it may be several days before they are able to speak. But they know all that is going on around them.

That is the strange story of the border-line state. The stories not only agree, but they relate the same understandable events.

Such are the marvelous secrets of God and Man and the Future Life, discovered by the Ancient Masters and taught to their disciples.

These Masters were so far ahead of us, that they recognized as a fact, and actually proved the existence of, man's Soul or Spirit. They termed it the "Ba," and drew pictures of it as a Dove, sometimes with a human head, hovering over the physical body in death.

This philosophy was regarded so highly by the church fathers, that they stole it from the Egyptians and had it appear in all of the four gospels: "The Holy Ghost descended in a bodily shape like a Dove upon him" (*Matthew 3:16; Mark 1: 10; Luke 3:22; John 1:32*).

Pictures of the "Ba" appear in the Egyptian Book of the Dead, in the text of which the deceased Ani is made to ask Ra, "How long have I to live?" Ra replies "Thou shalt exist for millions of millions of years," writes Budge, who adds: Thus is man "born again" into that "new life of the invisible world, which is beyond the grave and is everlasting." (Volume 2, page 141).

Life in the physical body is wonderful; and yet how grand is transition.

The levity of the body, the expanding space, the absence of time and darkness, the grandeur of the haze surrounding them, the capacity to see their physical body, showing the existence of the Spirit or Soul, of the dual consciousness, and proving that the Divine Consciousness is independent of the physical brain, of which 85 percent is only water.

This knowledge begins to lift the curtain and reveal the science and secrets of the Ancient Mysteries. By conducting the candidate to the very border-line state, "the abode of (physical) death" he was scientifically taught that when man dies physically, when the physical body (the Knat) dissolves, it rarely means that the permanent living spiritual man (the Ba) is withdrawn from the material counterpart, and that the Spiritual Double survives the event, and continues its eternal existence under spiritual conditions, in that "new life of the invisible world, which is beyond the grave and is everlasting."

Plutarch (46-125 AD) said that the religious rites of the Egyptian Mysteries not only taught that the Soul is immortal, but they proved it.

"O Mysteries most truly holy! O pure Light! Heaven and the Deity are displayed to my eyes (in the border-line state of transition!) I am initiated, and become holy! Hail New-Born Light! "

Such was held to be the effect of complete initiation into the Egyptian Mysteries (Pike, Freemasonry, 1871, page 522).

Chapter 10
The Ancient Mysteries

The essence of all mysteries consists in this: The conception of an unapproachable Being, infinite, eternal, unchanging, and that of a God of Nature whose manifold power is directly disclosed to the senses in the incessant cycle of creation, birth, life, and death.

Nature is as free from dogmatism as from tyranny. So the Ancient Masters not only adopted her lessons, but adhered to her methods of imparting them. They attempted to reach the understanding thru the eye; and the greater part of their religious teaching was conveyed thru this ancient and most impressive mode of exhibition or demonstration.

The Sacred Mysteries were an impressive drama, exhibiting some legend significant of Nature's cycle of changes, of the visible universe in which the Divinity is revealed.

Unlike the religion of books or creeds, these mystic dramas and performances were neither the reading of a lecture nor the delivery of a sermon, but the opening of a problem, implying neither exemption from research; nor hostility to philosophy. On the contrary, philosophy is the great Mystagogue or Arch-Expounder of symbolism. But the interpretations of the Grecian Philosophy of the old myths and symbols were, in many instances, as ill-founded as in others they are correct.

The Mysteries embraced the three great doctrines of Ancient Theology. They treated of God, Man and Nature. In symbolical forms the Mysteries exhibited THE ONE, of which the Manifold is an infinite illustration.

For its own benefit and support, modern theology teaches a great falsehood when it asserts that the ancients were idolaters and pagans. For, according to the Ancient Masters, a Great Soul, diffused everywhere, vivified all members of the incense body of the Universe; and Intelligence, equally great, directed and governed all its movements, and maintained the equal harmony that resulted therefrom.

Thus, the Unity of the Universe contained in itself two entities, the (1) Soul and the (2) Intelligence, which pervaded all its parts. They were to the Universe what Soul and Intelligence are to man. The doctrine of the Unity of God — in this sense — was taught from the days of Adam until it was crushed in the 4th Century by Constantine, and then degraded by terming the Ancient Masters idolaters and heathens.

What the Masters meant by real things was (1) invisible beings, genii, the faculties or powers of Nature. It included everything not a part of the visible world, which was termed, by way of contrast, (2) apparent existence.

The theory of Genni, or Powers of Nature, and its Forces, personified in the Mysteries, made part of the sacred science of initiation, and of that religious spectacle of different beings exhibited in the Sanctuary. It was an essential part of the lessons given the initiates, to teach them the relation of their own soul with universal Nature, the greatest of all lessons. It meant to dignify man in his own eyes, and teach him his place in the Universe.

So the whole system of the Universe was displayed in all its parts to the eyes of the initiate; and the symbolic Cave, which represented it, was   adorned and clothed with all the attributes of the Universe.

To the visible world of matter, so organized, endowed with a double force (active and passive), divided between light and darkness, moved by a living and intelligent Power, governed by Genii, who presided over its different parts, and whose nature and character are more lofty or low in proportion as they possess a greater or less portion of physical matter, — to that world descends the Soul, emanation of the ethereal fire, and exiled from the luminous region above the earth. The Soul enters into this dark matter. (physical substance), wherein the hostile principles, each seconded by its troops of Genii, are ever in conflict, there to submit to one or more organizations in the body that is its prison, until it shall at last be released from its prison by death (physical dissolution), so it may return to its high place or origin, its native habitat, from which, during earthly life, it is an exile.

Teaching this esoteric lesson to the Neophyte, the Masters shove to recall man to his divine origin, and indicated to him the means of returning thither. Thus, the natural science acquired in the Mysteries was a true knowledge of man's own self, of the nobleness of his origin, the grandeur of his destiny, and his superiority over the lower animals that can never acquire this higher knowledge, and yet which he resembles so long as he fails to rise above the animal plane by reflecting upon his own existence and sounding out the depths of his own nature.

By doing and suffering in his physical existence, man was finally released from his natural body and ascended along the path of the Milky Way, by the gate of Capricorn and the Seven Spheres, to a place whence, by gradations and successive lapses of consciousness and enthrallments, he (his soul) had descended.

Hence, the theory of the Spheres, and the signs and intelligences which preside there, and the whole system of astronomy, were scientifically connected with that of the Soul and its destiny, and symbolized in the Zodiac. These secrets of Nature were taught the Neophyte in the Mysteries, in which were developed the great principles of physics and metaphysics as to the origin of the Soul, its condition here below, its destination and future existence.

The Mysteries were divided into the Lesser and the Greater. One had to be an initiate of the Lesser for sorry years before being eligible for admission into the Greater. The Lesser was a school of preparation for the Greater, the Vestibule of the Temple. In the Lesser the candidate was prepared to receive the holy truths taught in the Greater. The initiates in the Lesser were called simply Mystes, or Initiates, in the Greater they were known as Epoptes, or Seers. The candidate being found worthy of admission into the Lesser Mysteries, the ceremony there commenced with an anthem to the Great God of Nature and then followed this apostrophe: "O mighty Being, greater than all other gods, we bow down before Thee as the primal Creator, Eternal God of gods. Thou art the Incorruptible Being, the Ancient Absolute Existence, the Supreme supporter of the Universe."

Being taught the first great primitive truth, the candidate was required to make a formal declaration, that he would be tractable and obedient to his superiors; that he would so live as to keep his body healthy and vigorous, govern his tongue, and observe a passive obedience in receiving the doctrines and traditions of the order; and the firmest secrecy in maintaining inviolable its hidden and abstruse mysteries.

In the Lesser Mysteries the initiate was taught 'lessons of morality, and the rudiments of the sacred sciences, the most sublime and secret parts of which were reserve — for the Epopt, who saw the Truth in its nakedness, whereas the Mystes viewed it only thru a veil and under emblems fitter to excite than to satisfy his curiosity. Most authors fix at five years the time required to elapse between admission from the Lesser to the Greater Mysteries.

When at length, after a long course of instruction, the candidate was admitted to the Degree of Perfection; he was brought face to face with entire Nature, and learned that the Soul is the real man; that the earth is but his place of exile; that heaven is his native home; that for the Soul to be born into 'the physical world is really to die; and that death is for it the return to its native country. Then he entered the sanctuary; but he did not receive the whole instruction at once. It continued thru several years. There were many departments, thru which he advanced by degrees, and between which thick veils intervened.

The book of Revelation, written by Apollonius, is a symbolic presentation of Cosmic Science and the secret of Regeneration that was taught in the Ancient mysteries. He purposely made the work so highly symbolical that the compilers of the New Testament, in the 4th Century lacked the knowledge of Nature to interpret it. For that reason the narrative remains practically unaltered and no modern clergyman is able to interpret it. Except for the first nine verses, added to the first chapter, and other fraudulent interpolations, made by the compilers of the New Testament to give the work the appearance of being "The Revelation of Jesus Christ," Few alterations have been made.

More secrets of physiology are concealed in the Revelation than modern science will know in a century from now. The Book of Seven Seals symbolizes the fact that Creative Cycles work thru sevens in the development and arrangement of form. The Masters discovered that the human body and the Universe are geometrical figures directly related, and that Sound and Number rule the Creative Processes.

The seven churches refer to the seven principle nerve plexi of the spinal cord. They are the Seven Spirits or chief centers thru which the etheric (atomic) energy functions (*Revelation 1:4*). The "opening of the Seven Seals" (*Revelation 5:5*) means the physiological awakening of these centers.

The biblical allegories relate always to the body and its physiology. Zechariah refers to these centers as the "seven eyes of the Lord," which run (flow) to and fro thru the whole earth (body -- 4:10). They are the "watchmen," and it is thru the awakening of these "eyes" that the great work of Regeneration is accomplished.

The Golden Candlestick that Zechariah saw (4:2) is the Spinal Column. The Silver Cord is the spinal cord (*Ecclesiastics 12:6*). The Golden Bowl (*Ecclesiastics 12:6*) upon the top of it, is the Brain, the seat of the emotions and ruler of the body's physiology. The Seven Lamps symbolize the Seven Nerve Centers, the function of which is to amplify the voltage of the regenerative process.

These disks of nerve plexi in the spinal cord resolve at tremendous speed, and produce spiritual light. The Seven Pipes (*Zechariah 4:2*) are the principle nerves that connect the plexi, and thru which the spiritual light rises into each nerve plexus to be amplified as the regenerative process progresses, until it reaches the Golden Bowl (brain), where Spiritual Illumination occurs, allegorically tented the "marriage of the Lamb" (*Revelation 19:7*). Physiologically speaking, this is the joining of the functions of the mysterious Pituitary and Pineal Glands in the Brain, the physiology of which modern science knows nothing.

In the Mysteries, baptism meant, among other things, the use of Holy Water, free from inorganic impurities that clog the Pituitary and Pineal Glands. The revivification of these strange glands was an important role in the instruction of the Neophyte. Holy Water meant pure rain water from the clouds, distilled by Nature and not contaminated with earthy matter.

Thus we discover that the biblical allegories not only refer to the body and its physiology, but that they can be interpreted only by an expert anatomist and physiologist who is far ahead of the great doctors of the day. Yet the dumb multitude walks in such darkness that people believe that health teaching should not be mixed and crossed with religious teaching.

These are some of the secrets taught in the Ancient Mysteries. But since the 4th Century the clergy has attempted to make these allegories refer to "Our Lord and Savior Jesus Christ," who "Washed us from our sins in his own blood" (*Revelation 1:15*).

Briefly, such were the Ancient Mysteries, the religious school of the Ancient Masters, — the work of which is more fully covered in our complete course of study, prepared from data gathered from the scattered and widely separated fragments that have come down to us in the precious ruins of the Temples of the Masters, who were so far ahead of us in wisdom that only now are we becoming able to interpret some of their marvelous symbols and parables.

Initiation was a great school of learning. It taught the sublime truths of existence and attributes of God, the immortality of the Soul, the phenomena of Nature, the arts and sciences, and those oral and written traditions briefly communicated which went back to the first ages of man.

"Pretextantus, Proconcul of Archaia," a man endowed with all the virtues, said in the 4th Century, when the destruction of the Ancient Mysteries was taking place, that –

"To deprive the world of the Sacred Mysteries which bound together the whole human race, would make life insupportable."

Nevertheless, the ancient institution of science and religion was destroyed. And when we consider the darkness into which that destruction plunged all of Europe, and what Europe has been since then, we can see haw true was that prophecy.

When Constantine crushed the Ancient Mysteries and established the Roman Catholic Hierarchy as the state religion, his theologians were directed to keep out of the New Testament all traces of the natural philosophy of the Masters. But that was impossible, as the New Testament was compiled from the scriptures of the Mysteries. That's the reason why it contains the remarkable philosophy of Apollonius, explaining the Born Again mystery (*1 Colossians 15*).

The human mind still speculates on the mysteries of Nature, as it gropes for Light in the darkness of modern civilization. It still finds that the latest discoveries of science were anticipated by the Masters, whose profoundest doctrines are to be searched for, not in their philosophies but in their symbols, by which they strove to express the deep theories that vainly struggled for utterance in words, as they pondered the mysterious cycle of phenomena. — Creation, Birth, Life, Death (or Decomposition), and New Life (Born Again) out of Death or Dissolution, — to them the greatest of mysteries.

Chapter 11
Spiritual Intuition (A)

"If a man die, shall he live again?" — *Job 14:14*.

That burning question has been put by the poet to all generations. It rises with the dawn of the race; and more time and money have been expended in searching for the answer, than for anything else on earth. All thru Life that thought haunts man. The world's destiny is composed of the issues of Life and Death. All human endeavors is ruled by the expectation of Death. The uncertainty that lies beyond Death more or less affects every man, every community, every nation.

The dread of Death is the bitter drop in the cup of Life. It is the dragon of our dreams, the despair of our days, the worry of our years. It strikes tenor to the heart of priest and peasant, savant and slave, bird and beast. The love of Life inspires every living creature.

Man alone has the intelligence to hope for Immortality. He longs to live after somatic death. He craves knowledge to support his hope and faith of a Future Life. Human hope and faith alternate with dread and doubt. Hope is not faith, and faith is now knowledge.

Hope for Immortalism is inseparable from human intelligence. It is the despair of king and servant, savage and sage. It is the theme of every sermon; the thread of every sacred song. Every book we read, every lesson we learn, brings man but one thought — Everlasting Life (*Psalm 90:2*). "The Immortality of Man" says Emerson, "is as legitimately preached from the intellections as from the moral volitions."

The most precious literature is that based upon the problem of a Future Life and the knowledge of its attainment. The sacred writings of ancient nations antedate secular history.

These solemn facts testify to the paramount importance of the subject, and justify the vigorous search throughout Nature for evidence and knowledge upon the subject.

The universal expectation of Immortality rises from conditions that are not physical. Had the Mind depended solely upon facts for the birth of the faith in a Future Life, it had never evolved. For no one who ever gazed upon a dead body could have conceived the thought of Immortalism.

Hope of Everlasting Life comes first as a purely Spiritual Intuition, which is not only universal, but as strong in the savage as in the sage. Yet physical science lightly dismisses that fact as "rank superstition." It was undoubtedly this Spiritual Intuition of the First Race that laid the foundation of religious worship. Theology rests upon Spiritual Intuition and faith therein.

Intuition is an all-significant phase of mental function that is rarely analyzed. Theology lacks the knowledge to analyze it, and physical science shuns it for fear of the findings that might result.

All acts of Intuition are acts of the Subconscious Mind, which occultism terns God Consciousness. Conscious mind is reasoning will. Subconscious mind directs the involuntary functions of the body, and is constantly in direct contact with Universal Mind.

Intuition signifies the natural endowment of knowledge, or knowledge from the Infinite Source received thru the subconscious mind.

Before the child is capable of intelligent reasoning, it is dependend upon this Inner Subconscious Self for its existence, and it is never misguided. All the Mind manifests at birth appears later in the adult as the Subconscious Mind. Acts of Intuition are acts of the Subconscious Mind, directed by Infinite.

Intelligence. It is Intuition that prompts the new-born-babe to inhale into its lungs the Breath of Life, and to seek food.

Long prior to Man's conscious conception of the source of supply, life, breath, health, strength, and all things necessary for his development were his Subconscious Possessions.

Spiritual Intuition declares to Man that Death does not end all. The Soul of Man rejects the scientific theory of annihilation. The Soul universally entertains hope or faith of a Future Life.

As this type of Intuition is universal, it is natural. Natural impulses imply a natural law of fulfillment. A natural desire that is universal, as the desire to breathe, drink and eat, implies a natural means of accomplishment. Universal tendencies are always based on universal principles.

It is as natural to desire immortality as to desire air, water, food, rest, and sleep. The Evolutionist who says that man is only an improved ape, that Death ends all, can hardly be said to live.

The Intuition of Immortality, while not proof to the cold calculations of physical science, is truth to man's intelligence. It is as much a part of Universal Truth as though it were capable of physical demonstration. For it is knowledge direct from the Infinite Source.

Man alone is capable of reasoning upon his own intuitions. He alone has the intelligence to seek a rational explanation of these intuitions. He alone is capable of demanding that the Cosmos shall yield up its secrets of these mysterious hopes, fears and expectations that alternately inspire and terrify the Soul.

The Spiritual Intuition of the savage established the expectation of the Future Life. The Masters solved by rational means the process of verify their own Intuitions.

We know the potency of inspiration or Spiritual Perceptions that are not explainable in cold reason. Intuition, while not knowledge to the Conscious Mind, is a higher guide than either cold reason or the Conscious Mind, especially such reason as that which entirely ignores the convictions of the Soul, which is a part of the Universal Soul from which Intuition flows.

Except for the natural expectation of Immortality, Man could not properly plan his destiny upon the physical plane. Faith is a perpetual inspiration; but modern skepticism clouds the best efforts. A creed of annihilation by the Materialists and Evolutionist saps the springs of human energy, and thwarts the highest possibilities. All visible things give Man many hints of Immortality. In winter, the hills and valleys seem chilled in death, held apparently lifeless by the grim hand of snow and ice. Every bud, twig, blade of grass is still. Is that death? Is that annihilation? Is that the end?

Then comes the spring, and as we stroll over these same regions we see throbbing Life everywhere. What has happened? The warm hand of the Solar God has touched the frozen hills and snow covered valleys, and lo and behold, they have risen into New Life as though by magic. Is Man less provided for than these things? In this fact is a startling hint that when the heart of Man ceases to beat and the body grows cold, his Higher Self will pass into New Life.

The nature and constitution of Man are the best evidence of Immortality. There is a universal longing to live on and on. Whence this longing? Is it only a delusion?

Man thirsts, and there are liquids to satisfy. He hungers, and there is food to satisfy. He tires, and there are rest and sleep to satisfy. It makes sense to hope that in like manner the higher longing will be satisfied. If the lower desires find satisfaction, shall the higher ones go unfilled?

If we turn to theology for the answer, we are sadly disappointed. If Christendom knew what it professes to believe, the whole existing order of its discourses and sermons would radically change.

If physical science were able to conceive that there might be facts of Nature beyond the scope and methods of its own school, then scientific study and research would include the Psychic Phenomena of Life.

Both theology and science agree in holding that human intelligence may not penetrate deeper into the secrets of Nature than we have gone.

The church professes faith in Immortality. But the practice of priest and preacher suggests more doubt than faith. If "I know" could replace "I believe" the whole dismal paraphernalia of Death would disappear.

If Christians had an unwavering faith in their dogmas, their lament for the dead would be greatly modified.

When Death claims his friend, the Christian mourner exhibits but little greater fortitude and faith than the average unbeliever or heretic. The Christian mourns his dead with an abandon that demonstrates the instability of his faith and declares the reality of his doubt.

If one firmly believes in Immortality, there is neither reason nor excuse for this intemperate grief.

If man could know what he but mournfully hopes rather than believes, the House of Death would not be a House of Despair. Instead it would be a House of Joy whenever Death released the Spirit from decrepitude and misery. If woman possessed the faith they pretend, they could not swathe themselves with mourning crepe, nor visit cemeteries to commune with the Dead that are not there.

If theology could rationally demonstrate a basis for its faith, Life would be transformed with new inspirations and higher aspirations. If physical science could prove its major promise, that "all is physical matter and mechanical energy," the Church would disintegrate within a year.

Theology makes no rational attempt to verify its faith in Immortality, because it is utterly ignorant of the true Law of Animation, and is grossly ignorant of physical facts and the state of Spirituality.

If physical science could discover the true Law of Animation, it would realize that Life Eternal is as certain as is the indestructibility of Matter. Physical science simply scorns the suggestion of Spirituality, while it conducts a vigorous campaign against what it glibly terms the "superstitions of humanity."

It is far easier to conceive that physical science has not been in position to demonstrate all the facts of Nature, than to doubt all the Spiritual Philosophy of the world. The weakness of theology is its ignorance of physical and spiritual facts. The weakness of physical science is its ignorance of the true Law of Life.

Both systems, being human, are narrow and prejudiced. Each is jealous of the other, and each quickly suppresses all apparent facts that tend to upset its theories, while it liquidates and silences all those who refuse to be limited and bound by its dogmas and doctrines.

Chapter 12
Spiritual Intuition (B)

With all the boasted progress of science and invention, for the last thousand years man has lived in darkness as dense as ever as to his origin and destiny, the operation of his Mind, the Life Principle, the Principle of Intelligence, his relation to God and the Universe, and many other things.

Romanism and materialism are the obstacles in the path of progress. Romanism has crushed the spiritual intuition in man, and physical science regards man as only a material machine.

When modern physics exploded with the discovery of the electron, it attempted to "save face" by conceiving the electron as existing in the sane artificial world ruled by Aristotelian and Newtonian laws, in which visible phenomena is studied.

The electron has been accepted and considered by modern physics as existing in the same world in which exist our bodies and other objects commensurable with them. It refuses to understand or believe that electrons belong to another world.

The Masters taught that man evolves from the Spiritual World into the Physical World, clad in garments of clay, with a purpose that extends beyond the grave. Modern science holds that man is only a material machine, and that everything ends for him at the grave.

1. One of the properties in Absolutism is Intelligence (Law). Cosmic Intelligence inheres by nature in all things and interpenetrates all particles of spiritual and physical substance.

Cosmic Intelligence appears in Men as Individual Intelligence which he thinks is his own and of himself. As a Form of Clay, he has no Intelligence. That Intelligence which he thinks is of himself, is his individualized and limitized expression of Cosmic Intelligence.

2.   Another one of the properties in Absolutism is Consciousness. Cosmic Consciousness also inheres by nature in and interpenetrates every living thing, and every particle of every living thing. As a Form of Clay, man has no Consciousness. That Consciousness which he thinks is of himself, is his individualized and limitized expression of Cosmic Consciousness.

Fundamental Truths of the Universe come to man thru those Cosmic channels, and appear in him as Spiritual Intuition. This faculty has been crushed and dramatized in civilized man by despots for their profit and power. It is more active in primitive races because they have more freedom and less suppression by their rulers.

Intuition is involuntary urgings and promptings, received in Man's conscience without apparent effort. It is the effect of Cosmic Consciousness flowing into the brain, and informing man that he is more than Potter's Clay (*Job 33:6*).

These facts must be kept hidden from the multitude. To let the masses know these things is dangerous to organized institutions, but less dangerous now than when Papal power was supreme.

Doctor Carver writes, "We are limited in our acquisition of knowledge to intuition — deductions. There is no other, there has never been another, there will never be another channel thru which we may receive Universal Intelligence. We must get Universal Truth, if at all, thru intuition."

It is not beyond the grave, nor in the distant regions of the Universe, nor in physical man, that we should search for the solution of the secret of what occurs in Somatic death.

The answer is found in many places, including the Bible, which says, Man is transformed; he is changed in the twinkling of an eye (in the process termed death), and his Real Self is released, from its physical prison and passes to a new environment, a new state of consciousness, in the Future Life, where new wonders greet him (*1 Corinthians 15:51, 52*).

The Solar Spirit in man is termed the Soul, and a vague consciousness, coming from the Infinite, has informed the lowest of men thru the Soul, that he is more than mortal.

This vague consciousness affects the sub-conscious power in man, and appears in him as Spiritual Intuition. Modern science terms it "superstition," while Romanism calls it "heresy."

By theology man is taught to believe in a God in a remote region ruling in a mythical heaven, with the gospel Jesus sitting on His right hand (*Mark 16:19*). This theory was invented to enslave man and keep him in darkness. Man's subconscious mind, ruling the involuntary functions of his body, is the link that connects Conscious Man with Cosmic Consciousness.

The intelligence of the subconscious mind is far greater than that of the conscious mind. The subconscious mind is ruled by Universal Intelligence, whereas the conscious mind is ruled by man's five physical senses.

Suppose we should imagine faithfully that we are actually Eternal Life. We continue this psychic state until a neurosis or brain path is formed. Then the idea becomes fixed and functions in our subconscious mind constantly. Exhilarating vibrations are produced which affect the blood and vital organs, and we begin to progress to a higher plane of consciousness.

When you commence to do this, reveal the secret to no one. for the reaction of friends would be unfavorable, and you would be regarded as a fool or a liar. We hate those who rise above us and pity those who fall below us. Various means are employed to keep us in darkness. We are steeped in scientific materialism, in the theory of evolutionism, in the church dogma of super-naturalism, and in what not isms?

So we logically live in fear of strange impressions that come to us, and reject the inner urge, the peculiar pressure on our intuition, our instinct, and conceal from friends the strange missions that actually come to us from the Spiritual World. If we revealed them, we would be adjudged "possessed" or insane.

Not so many years ago. the world was filled with "witches." This was another fraud of Romanism. When it saw its power fading as a result of the bold work begun by Luther, it grew more desperate and resorted to more bloody deeds to hold its victims in line.

Witchcraft was one of these measures. It painted a terrifying picture of "witches" who were alleged to be certain people who believed that there was a King Devil, and that he sent forth millions of lesser imps that entered into the bodies of men and women who were willing to make the requisite compact in order that they might do injury to their enemies. Darkness is necessary to make people believe such fraud.

In the terrible 16th Century, Romanism urged the criminal prosecution of "witches"" by the civil authorities, composed of men who feared the power of the Romanists.

"Witch hunts" became common. People were afraid to show any unusual intelligence, or internal feelings, or inner impressions that came to them and women in particular, always more psychic than man, feared to incur the displeasure of friends and neighbors, knowing they might be charged with endeavoring to "cast a spell" over them, or with having formed a compact with Satan.

By the 17th Century the masses of Europe had been taught by Romanism to hunt for "witches" and thousands of innocent persons were tried, convicted by courts ruled by Romanism, and put to death. John Wesley (1705-1791), a "big shot" Romanist in England, declared that "to disbelieve in witchcraft is to disbelieve in the Bible." In England more than 30,000 "witches"" were burned at the stake. The last victim was executed in Scotland in 1722. In 1670 such executions were forbidden in France by official edict issued by Louis XIV. In England the prosecution of "witches" was abolished by act of Parliament in 1736.

In glorious America the last execution of "witches" occurred in 1692. The Pilgrim Fathers fled from Europe to the wilderness of America in 1620 to escape from Roman persecution, but they took with them some of their "Roman superstition." Romanism begins to decline when Spiritual Intuition is allowed to live.

Man must be kept in mental slavery and darkness to save Romanism. He must consider himself fortunate if he can safely hope to reach Purgatory after he dies. hence the almost constant pre-occupation of Romanites with their fate beyond the grave.

The specter of the dead is forever present in the controlled mind of the Romanite, along with the great fear that his repeated works of penance and obedience to the priest's command will not even get him to Purgatory. His unquestioning dependence upon the priest as his mediator with God can thus be understood. Mental enslavement is the answer.

Only in more recent times has it become safer, not safe, for psychic phenomena to be brought out of the darkness, and for literature like this work to see the light of day.

Man is slowly breaking the chains of Roman darkness, and returning to the path trod by the Masters — but at what unspeakable terror, horror, blood-shed and cost.

Due to persecution, civilized man has been afraid to develop his Inner Power of Mind sufficiently to realize that the demise of his body does not damage his Spiritual Self.

In recent years, with the invention of radio, it has become more difficult for Romanism to suppress knowledge of the Spiritual World — knowledge to the effect that the seemingly silent and empty Ether is really another world by which we are unconsciously surrounded, and which is saturated with sounds, awaiting only the proper instruments to make them audible to man.

Then comes television, and images are added to sound. This proves that the Image of persons and other objects, as well as sound, is projected thru space at terrific speed.

Within the short space of our own time, the mystery of the Spiritual World, so long suppressed by Romanism, and so long scorned by materialism, and so well explored by the Masters, has been slightly revealed to us.

More amazing mysteries of the Spiritual World are yet to come, as we gain more freedom from the suppression of Romanism and materialism, and advance in knowledge of Spiritual Truth.

Even now, telepathy is a proven fact. But civilized man's mental processes are so faulty, due to suppression and degeneracy, that this faculty must be improved by the improvement of man's brain and body, in order to bring him up nearer to the physical state of that of the Masters. Then his brain will become capable of better function.

Chapter 13
Esoteric Knowledge

Consciousness is defined as the knowledge of sensations and rental operations, certain knowledge from observation or experience.

That definition describes only man's expression of Consciousness.

Atomic expression of Consciousness is omniscient, omnipresent and Omni prevalent, filling all in both the visible and invisible worlds, filling every plant and tree, every cell of the human body, and every molecule, atom and electron in the human cells and in the whole Cosmos. The Consciousness of men appears as an emanation of Cosmic Consciousness, limited in man by his cerebral capacity. Cosmic Consciousness contains a complete record of all atomic existence, each atom being a solar system in itself, containing stars, satellites and planets, on all of which are engraved the events extending from the present of the most remote past.

Man's consciousness should therefore contain a record of his entire existence. But in his physical state his previous existence fades out of his physical consciousness. In rare cases some men faintly recollect dim impressions of fragments of their previous life, and that knowledge is an enigma to them. If they mention the fact to friends in the hope of receiving some help to explain it, they are regarded as fools or liars.

Every event is the result of some event that caused it. No event can originate itself. Each act that enters into man's existence is one link in the continuous chain that extends back to the time when man first appeared on earth. Man is not able to originate an act or an event. All that he does is the result of what has preceded him. Man is not a producer in the cosmic sense. He cannot produce his own thoughts. What he thinks is what comes to him in the endless chain of causation, or cause and effect. What he does is a series of acts, all of which have resulted from other acts preceding, and not one of which he has been able to originate or produce. One of the greatest philosophers of the preceding generation, and an astronomer of note, Richard A. Proctor, declared that every mundane event is controlled by an endless line of causations reaching back to the time when the earth was a cloud of dust in the sky.

These chains of causation are said by leading psychologists to be recorded in the atomic worlds of the Meninges, or enveloping membranes of the brain and spinal cord.

In a pound of the Meninges there are several thousand grains. In a pound of grain, or one part of seventy thousand parts of a pound, there are 90,000 billions of atoms. Each atom is a solar system of its own, having planets and satellites, each containing approximately 150,000 ions. Recorded here are the events of a past that stretches back so far as to take on the attribute of eternity. Here an omniscient mind may read the past and the future.

Concerning this, Proctor wrote: "Every event, let its direct importance be what it may, is indissolubly bound up with events preceding, accompanying, and following it, in endless series of causation, interaction and effect."

Unless there is some psychological interference intervening, these events will proceed forward as they have come out of the past, bound up, as Proctor says, in endless series.

As stated above, in addition to the common state of human consciousness, it has been established that there are other states, which are rare and which have been studied very little in modern times.

It is in these rare states, where some persons faintly remember dim impressions of fragments of their previous life, that we can learn and understand that which we cannot learn and understand in our ordinary state of consciousness. This in its turn serves to establish the fact that the ordinary state of consciousness is only a particular instance of consciousness and that our ordinary conception of the world is only a particular instance of conception of the world.

Mysticism may be considered as a projection of hidden knowledge into our ordinary state of consciousness; and those who receive such knowledge will do well to keep silent about it, or they may be regarded with suspicion. Mysticism could not exist without hidden knowledge, and the theory of hidden knowledge could not be known without mysticism. Occult science says that the whole of knowledge is contained within the Soul of man, as stated above. Hidden knowledge is an idea that does not fit into any idea, and the suggestion is rejected by science.

If we follow neither the religious nor the scientific view, but try to compare descriptions of the mystical experiences of entirely different races, different periods and different religions, we find a remarkable resemblance in these descriptions, which can in no case be explained by similarity of preparation or by resemblances in ways of thinking and feeling.

In mystical states, utterly different people in utterly different conditions learn one and the same thing, and, what is still more striking, in mystical states there is no difference of religions. All the experiences are absolutely identical; the differences being only in language and form of the description. In the mysticism of different countries and different peoples, the same images, the same discoveries, are invariably repeated.

Humanity is regarded by occultism as two concentric circles. All the history of humanity that we know, is the history of the outer circle. Within the outer circle there is another circle, of which men of the outer circle know nothing, and the existence of which they sometimes only dimly suspect. Yet the life of the outer circle in its most important manifestations, and particularly in its development, is actually guided by the inner circle. The inner or esoteric circle forms a life within a life.

Modern science is completely materialistic, and materialism grew out of Romanism. The ancient world was never superficially materialistic. The Masters regarded the Material as only a vehicle for the Spiritual (*1 Corinthians 6:19*). The Masters knew how to penetrate to the depths of an idea, and how to find in it not only one meaning, but many meanings. We hear much and know little of the higher mind and higher consciousness. The idea of esotericism is chiefly that of the higher mind. To realize what this means, we must first understand that ordinary minds are not the highest possible order of mind.

Human thought can work on very different levels. The human mind can rise to levels almost inconceivable to the ordinary mind, and we can see the results of the work of higher mind — those most accessible to us being the astonishing allegorism and the astounding symbolism of the Ancient Masters, appearing in the Bible and in other ancient literature, and on the stone temples and monuments of the ancient world.

The Masters regarded the earth, moon and sun as symbols of material, psychic and divine objects, and recognized the fact that there are corresponding states of consciousness, graded according to the degree to which mental possibilities are realized. These can also be classed as material, psychic and divine.

The Masters held that integral reality comprises an identifiable series of discontinuous realms, some of which are normally imperceptible to the average man. Every person has the latent potentiality for developing a corresponding series of faculties with which he can contact and know these higher realms.

Some persons are more fortunate than others in being born with or in acquiring various degrees of higher perceptive powers, such as telaesthesia, prescient dreams, telepathy, television. Others develop a higher and rarer faculty of insight and become transcendental philosophers, prophetic seers or mystics.

The first step in comprehending the idea of esotericism is the realization of the existence of a higher mind — a mind that differs from the ordinary mind as much as the mind of an intelligent and educated adult differs from the mind of a child of six. The Master with the higher mind possesses knowledge unknown to ordinary man, however clever and intelligent he may be. This is termed esoteric knowledge. The logical mind knows its limitations and is strong enough to resist the temptation to venture, without proper training, into problems beyond its powers and capacities, and thus becomes a psychological mind.

The method used by the psychological mind is that of distinguishing between different levels of thinking, and of realizing the fact that perceptions change according to the towers and properties of the perceiving faculty. The psychological mind can see the limitations of the "logical mind" and the absurdities of the "defective mind". It can understand the realities of the existence of a higher mind and of esoteric knowledge, and see it in its manifestations. That is impossible for a merely logical mind.

Scientists of the logical mind demand physical demonstration for everything, yet such demonstration of great truths appears only in the effects produced by Cosmic Causes — in the products of the unseen Intelligence and Force that direct and produce that visible world which men call Nature.

The depths hidden within men's conscious mind were well understood by the Masters, who taught that everything is within man, and there is nothing outside him (*Luke 17:21*).

The Masters taught that by penetrating properly within the depths of himself, man may find everything and attain everything which he needs and which God intended for him to have. What he will attain depends on what and how he seeks (*1 Kings 4:33; Matthew 6:6*).

In common civilized life, man is oppressed, suppressed, misled, miseducated, deceived, kept in darkness, lives only on the surface of himself, and is, accordingly, ignorant and even unconscious of what lies in his own depths — in the billions of solar systems of the atoms of his body and brain, on which are recorded the events of his being from the present back to eternity.

Before the physical world existed in its present form, man was (*John 8:58*). But when misled civilized man thinks of infinity, he is taught to conceive it as being outside him. The Masters knew and taught that infinity is within man. By consciously and silently penetrating within his own Soul, man may there find infinity within himself, come in contact with it, and enter into it. That is Cosmic Consciousness.

"Man has become so earthly and outward," wrote Gichtel, a mystic of the 17th Century, "that he seeks afar, deep in the starry sky, in the higher eternity (as modern science is doing), for that which is quite near him, within the inner center of his Soul."

The more the Soul penetrates within itself, the nearer it approaches God, until it finally appears before the Holy Trinity, where it reaches the deeper and hidden knowledge.

The peculiarity and the distinctive features of the ideas of the Real World appear absurd when considered in the light of modern materialism. We hear much about Superman and are led to believe that the nearness or remoteness of Superman from man lies in time. But it actually lies in man himself.

Man is not separated from Superman by time, but by himself. He is not ready to receive Superman. His Mind is closed by false teaching that prevents the entry of the hidden knowledge which transform man to Superman. In this world of organized fraud, Superman is an unlawful being. He violates the general course and condition of things. When he would appear, he is summarily silenced and liquidated. He is dangerous to modern establishments, to institutionalized religion, to limitized materialism, to scientificized evolutionism.

"I want to teach men the sense of their existence, which is the Superman, the lightning out of the dark cloud — man" (Thus Spake Zarathustra).

Chapter 14
Dormant Organs (A)

SON OF PERFECTION -

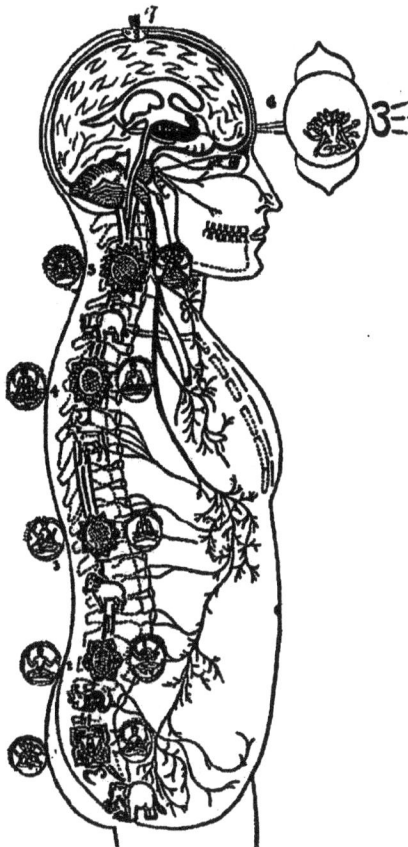

We must know anatomy, physiology, psychology and biology to know the human body and its functions, and to understand the biblical allegories. We must know more. We must know that the body of civilized man now contains many withered and dormant organs, the functions of which medical art knows nothing at all.

The majority of manuals including man, possess in the ears a radiogeniometric receiver, formed by the semi-circular canals arranged in three planes of space. This assemblage constitutes the labyrinth, a name given to a series of cavities in the internal ear, which is completed by the three more or less developed organs called the vestibule, the cochlea and the semi-circular canals.

The vestibule is an oval cavity in the internal ear that forms the entrance to the cochlea.

The cochlea is a cavity resembling a snail-shell. It consists of a tapering spiral tube, the inner wall of which is forged by a central column of modulus, around which it winds.

The semi-circular canals contain a superfine fluid that is particularly sensitive to electro-magnetic waves. The walls of the canals consist of insulating material.

The conducting fluid in the canals constitutes a directional receiving circuit, completed by an accessory circuit in the form of a pliable spiral (self-inductance) and capacity (condenser). Thus these canals in the ears are susceptible of playing the part of a radiogenic-metric receiver when developed to a functional degree, as they were in the Ancient Masters, but not in the great majority of civilized people.

A catarrhal condition, due to the polluted air and poisonous fumes of civilization, has practically destroyed the function of these canals in the ears of civilized man.

This is one of the secrets of the "weird Power" exhibited by the Indians of South America, whose mystifying feats were mentioned in a previous lesson. They had not experienced those "blessings" of civilization that degenerate man's body while making him believe they are helping him.

These special organs constitute an oscillating circuit far more powerful than that of the tiny cells of the body; and when contacted by electro-magnetic vibrations from the air, a series of powerful oscillations result. By the aid of these special directing organs, designed to pick up radiations, animals, and also men who are normal, become aware of vibrations for which they are searching. This is the scientific solution of the puzzling problem of so-called animal instinct.

Certain experiments with animals prove that the semi-circular canals in the ears are endowed with special directing properties. If these organs are removed in the case of birds, the birds lose their sense of equilibrium and turn round (continued the page 86)...

The Vital Battery

"There is nothing covered, that shall not
be revealed; and nothing hid, that shall not be known."
(Matthew 10:26)

The remarkable success of Chiropractic is due to the fact that the manipulations of the spinal column by the Chiropractor stimulate the cells of the battery and increase the flow of cosmic electricity (nerve force) to the various organs and glands.

This mysterious Battery with its Seven Cells is mentioned in the Bible as a Book with Seven Seals *(Revelation 5)*, but no priest nor preacher ever attempts to make a rational explanation of these Seven Seals. He knows as little about these Seven Seals as the man in the street.

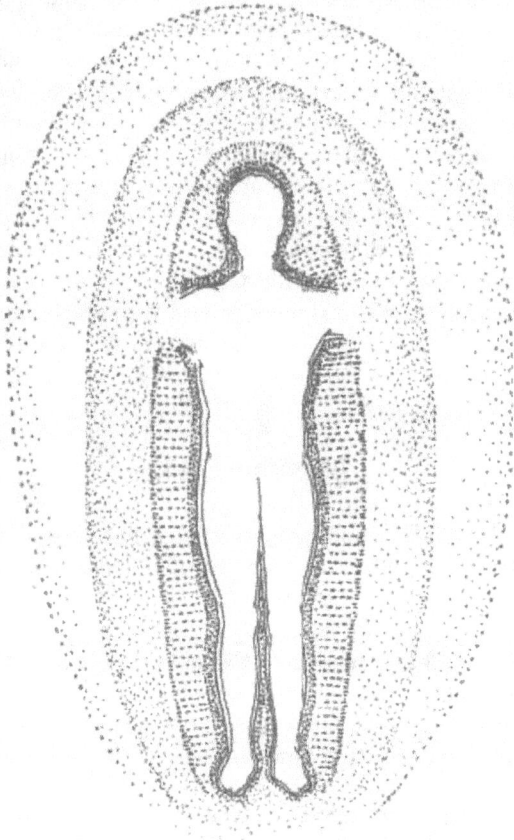

All traces of this the greatest secret of the body might have been lost to the Western World, had that precious Hindu Scroll not been included in the Bible. And to this day the church is unaware of the fact that a chart of this battery and its cells is concealed in Revelation.

Seven Sense Powers

Science says man has five sense powers, but the Ancient Masters taught and proved that he has Seven. That is another secret of the Vital Battery concealed in Revelation, the Book of Sevens.

When the multitude was feasted on Five Loaves and Two Fishes, the Five Loaves symbolized the Five Senses of the average man, and the Two Fishes symbolized the Two Higher Sense Powers of the Master. (*Matthew 14:17*).

After the feast "they took up of the fragments that remained 12 baskets full" (*Matthew 14:20*). The 12 baskets symbolized the 12 signs of the Zodiac.

Heed not the dead letter of the Bible. Look for the hidden meaning. The dead letter does not make sense, while the hidden meaning reveals the deeper secrets of Life.

There are two special glands in the brain and two in the body that are the main Cells of the Vital Battery, and Five Solaristic   Chambers   in the   head,   harmonious   and synchronous, man rises to the state of Seer-ship, Cosmic Consciousness.

... (continued from page 84) and round as though stupefied and incapable of taking a definite direction.

The octopus is still able to swim after being blinded, but turns round its longitudinal axis or plane of symmetry when the vesicles that control its faculty of orientation have been destroyed.

After the destruction of both labyrinths, aquatic animals and not ably frogs, can no longer swim or jump in a straight line.

Many insects possess minute antennae enabling them to follow their course in a bee-line toward distant points. These antennae exist only for the purpose of receiving radiations, and their loss or injury seriously handicaps the insects.

When considered clairvoyantly, the human body symbolizes a bouquet of flowers. For all over the body are located petal-like groups of emanating radiation.

One of these nerve centers is contained in the palms of the hands, and another in the soles of the feet. All the vital organs have whirling points of light as spiritual bases. These revolving points are important spiritual centers, and each of them, under certain conditions, is capable of aiding man to develop a much greater degree of consciousness. But he must first improve the general condition of his body by a better course of living in harmony with Cosmic Law.

It is possible for a normal man to see with the palms of the hands and the soles of the feet. But where will we find a normal man? The Ancient Masters could see with all parts of the body. A symbol of this condition appeared in the Egyptian Mysteries in the figure of Osiris, who was often shown sitting upon a throne, his whole body composed of eyes. Man is a creature of vibratory impressions only. That makes modern man's world of consciousness very small in his present degenerate state, with only five physical senses with which to contact the radiations and vibrations of the Universe, and these senses more or less defective.

Naturalists tell us that there are perhaps five hundred other senses employed by bugs, birds and beasts.

Consider man in a faint, or unconscious from drugs or anesthetic or injury. His body otherwise functions with the normal activities to maintain physical life. All that is absent is a state of physical consciousness. The subconscious mind of the real inner (spiritual) man is intact, uninjured, unchanged, and active. It is only the physical aspect of the conscious mind that is changed, inactive, as a result of which the open eyes can see nothing, the ears can hear nothing, and the physical senses of smelling, tasting, and feeling are absent. With his five physical faculties inactive, closed, and shut off from receiving any vibratory impressions conveying intelligence of the physical world, and also being unable to send forth any messages, the conscious mind of physical man is closed to all physical existence. This man is literally dead while he lives, so far as his conscious contact with the physical world is concerned.

Physical man in a state of physical unconsciousness knows absolutely nothing so far as the physical world is concerned. If he were actually dead, he could not know less of his earthly environment. Yet his physical body functions as if nothing had happened. He lives physically, but the physical aspect of his mind is totally blank. While in that state, he could enter the spiritual world and return from it, but never know it. In fact, he could be living in the spiritual world all the time — and be unaware of it.

These assertions are statements of facts. They seem startling to him in mental darkness who confesses his "sins" to the priest may be sure that he remains in mental darkness.

"Except a men be born of water and of the Spirit, he cannot enter into the kingdom of God" (*John 3:5*). Yet the Luke definitely states that "The kingdom of God is within you" (*Luke 17:21*).

Occult science asserts that man lives here, now and always in the kingdom of God. That kingdom embraces everything and includes all, both the physical and the spiritual world.

Man always lives in God's kingdom, but is physically unconscious of the fact because organized institutions of fraud and oppression, established to enslave the masses, have crushed that Eternal Knowledge out of his physical consciousness by controlling his Mind to prevent its normal development and to keep him in darkness.

Psychologists declare that civilized man rarely develops more than ten per cent of his normal brain capacity, while only five per cent of the people ever think for themselves.

The findings of these psychologists show that about ten per cent of the people are trying to think, but are blinded by their prejudices, and the rest are content to avoid the responsibility of thinking and are heedlessly following their leaders whose only interest is to gain power and hold it. Due to the rigidly controlled educational and religious systems of civilization, man is kept in darkness. The consciousness of this man is narrow and restricted, and is bound up with his earthly environment to the total exclusion of his spiritual environment.

There is one world with two aspects, the spiritual and the physical, and Man actually but unconsciously, lives in the spiritual world here and now.

Physical Man contacts the physical world with his physical senses, and spiritual man contacts the spiritual world with his spiritual senses.

The five spiritual faculties of modern man, of which his five physical senses are only the exteriorized products, are dormant, closed, inactive, shut off from receiving any vibratory impressions conveying intelligence of the spiritual world.

To modern man, with five defective physical senses and five dormant spiritual senses, there is no spiritual world and only a very small physical world.

How can we make him aware of that fact? How can we prevent organized institutions, for profit and power, from keeping man in mental darkness? How can we make man realize that he has a form of consciousness, in a dormant state, which no longer can perceive, or remember, the character of its own relation to the physical body? His mind is so well controlled and darkened by organized institutions that he refuses to believe these things when told; and material science, to "save face" and protect its reputation, bitterly scorns the idea when it is mentioned.

To man with his whole body properly developed as it should be, and in tune with the Infinite as it was intended to be, there is, but now in a dormant state, the Department of External Knowledge, which caused the Masters to write that there is nothing covered and nothing hidden that shall not be known (*Matthew 10:26*). Just as the physical world is an expression of the spiritual world, so man's physical senses are an expression of his spiritual senses.

Just as material science believes and teaches that the physical world includes all things and all power, so man is taught to believe that his physical senses include all the powers and faculties of his organism.

The Masters were not bound by false teaching and mental chains. They discovered that the physical senses arise as an expression of the spiritual senses, and by searching within for the Department of External Knowledge they found it. Modern man in mental darkness, with his mind and thinking controlled by organized institutions, searches without for Eternal Knowledge and never finds it.

Physical scientists search for it with microscope and telescope and declare it is all a myth of the "ancient heathens" because they cannot locate it. In order for man to develop consciousness on the higher plane, Buddhi needs the more differentiated fire of Manas, the details of which we have explained in THE MAGIC WAND. When the sixth sense (Manas) has awakened the seventh (Buddhi), the spiritual light radiating from the seventh illuminates the Fields of Infinitude in man's physical consciousness, and his Spiritual Consciousness, being thus aroused from its dormant state in the Third Resurrection, becomes active; and for that period of time man becomes omniscient. The Past and the Future, Space and Time, disappear and become for him the Present.

Chapter 15
Dormant Organs (B)

Organs in a rudimentary (dormant) condition in man, plainly shows that an earlier or prior progenitor possessed these organs in a fully developed, perfect and functional condition, and that this implies an enormous amount of modification in the descendants thereof. (Darwin, *Origin of Species*).

Physiologists know little concerning the functions performed by the various active organs of the body, and nothing at all of the functions formerly performed by the organs in the body that are now rudimentary and dormant. Medical art tries to hide its ignorance by regarding these dormant organs as 'hang-over-appendages" that were useful when man was in the ape-stage, guided by "animal instinct," useless to him now because he is guided by "superior intelligence."

Individualized intelligence is never superior to that phase of Eternal Intelligence which appears in animals and is termed "instinct." Instinct never leads an animal astray, whereas man's "superior" (individualized) intelligence is constantly leading him astray. We mentioned the radio-goniometric receiver in the ears of birds and beasts that enable them to determine their bearings unerringly during long voyages. They depend not on physical sight nor physical consciousness, but on Eternal Intelligence that operates through these special sense organs.

This power was given to man, but degeneration has destroyed it. The polluted air he breathes constantly, enters the Eustachian tube leading from the throat to the internal ear, and ear-ache in the small child is one signal that damage, being done to the internal ear, is destroying the delicate spiritual centers there. Occult science shows that the Intellectual Organs in man are those situated near the point where the nose joins the forehead. The small glands that cluster round this center have the peculiarity that they all relate to phenomena external to the body.

The five sinuses in the head-bones, the functions of which physical science knows nothing, are connected with the interior of the nose by short, narrow channels. Occult science teaches that these sinuses are spiritual chambers, in which is located the Throne of the Intellectual Divinity in Men.

Into these spiritual chambers there enters with the Breath of Life, a peculiar gaseous substance, a subtil essence, known to the Masters as Mental Spirit (*John 4:24; 6:63*).

This Divine Essence can no longer produce normal reactions in the spiritual chambers (sinuses) of civilized man, for they have been ruined and reduced to a dormant state by the destructive action of polluted air. In the biblical allegories, not understood by the clergy, this is the Paradise of the Sacred Desert (Brain); connected with the lower world (animal body) by the Rainbow or the Silver (Spinal) Cord, ascending from the Sacral Plexus to the Golden Bowl (Skull). (*Ecclesiastics 12:6*).

To these spiritual Chambers within the Golden Bowl the Masters taught their disciples to rise in their consciousness. This leads again to the Third Resurrection, twice before mentioned, in which the Neophyte, rising in consciousness from the lower man (animal nature) and the material world, ascends consciously into the Higher Man, the Brain, the Throne in the Temple of God (*1 Corinthians 3:17*). This is one of the top secrets of Ancient Science.

In the early days, when man was normal, the sinuses in his head and the labyrinths in his ears were particularly sensitive to the electro-magnetic vibrations of the Cosmos, and they were capable of performing the part of a radiogenic: metric receiver, by means of which the Masters acquired arcane knowledge of the Fourth Dimension.

Due to the functional development of these oscillating circuits in their splendid organisms, which things are allegorically referred to often in ancient scriptures, the Masters were in the same category that birds and beasts now are, with reference to these higher powers. It is reasonable to assure that they were on a still higher plane in their consciousness.

The special sense organs in their bodies were normal and in sympathetic vibration with the Cosmic Rays, hence the Masters could travel in a direct line, as birds now do, toward a distant goal that would be invisible and unknown to us. For they were capable of detecting vibrations which our dulled and dormant organs cannot perceive, thanks to civilization, polluted air, medical art, "medicine," doctors and degeneration.

When such incidents do occasionally occur among men, we call it instinct, intuition, insight. The Masters termed it Infinite Intelligence direct from the Cosmic Source. Romanism calls it the   work of Satan, and used to burn such victims at the iron stake.

Physical science and the modern clergy know not that the interpretation of the first six chapters of Genesis of the Bible, and the ancient history of men, are concealed in his own body, and there preserved forever in the dormant, rudimentary organs, the embryological and homologues structures remaining in the Temple of God. That which hath been is that which shall be again (*Ecclesiastics 1:9*).

Physical science has been so badly blinded by its theories of Materialism and Evolutionism, that it has scorned all suggestions to investigate these signs of Mother Nature and try to discover their hidden meaning. The dormant and rudimentary structures in man's body are only sleeping; they are not dead. They are capable of rebirth, resurrection, redevelopment and rehabilitation. When resurrected, they will bring forth that original Super Man that was originally created.

It is not in the works of the philosophers, but in the religious symbols of the Masters that we should look for the footprints of Cosmic Science, and re-discover the Mysteries of Man.

The Cosmic Science of the Ancient Magi (*Matthew 2:1*) was concealed from the profane in the temples of the Ancient Mysteries. The dogmas of this science were engraven in symbols on the tablets of stone of the Masters. Moses or someone else later re-veiled them, for that is the root-meaning of the word "reveal." He covered them deeper with a new veil to conceal them more securely from the despots when he made the Kabala the exclusive heritage of the Israelites and the inviolable secrets of the priests.

The Masters of Ancient Egypt knew far better than modern science the laws of movement and of life. They knew how to temper or intensify action by re-action; and they readily foresaw the realization of these effects, the causes of which they had determined. The Columns of Seth, Enoch, Noah, Shem, Solomon and Hercules have symbolized in Magian traditions this Cosmic Law of Equilibrium; and the Science of Equilibrium, or the balancing of forces, had led the Masters to that cosmic attraction, termed gravitation, round the centers of Life, Light and Heat.

Catholic authors and authorities have controlled history for 1600 years, and have diligently endeavored to conceal the fact that the most celebrated of the Greek philosophers gained their wisdom in the Egyptian Mystery Schools. Such; noted Greeks as Thales (640 B.C.), Solon (638 B.C.), Pythagoras (586 B.C.), Socrates (471 (B.C.), Democritus (470 B.C.), and Plato (427 B.C.), went to Egypt and were initiated into the Mystery Schools. Democritus, considered one of the greatest of the Greek philosophers, spent seven years there studying under the Egyptian Masters. Dean Dudley wrote that "Pythagoras lied when he said that his knowledge came directly as a revelation from God. For he received it from the Egyptian Priests, under whom he studied for 22 years."

Romanism so thoroughly destroyed the history and records of ancient Egypt, that much of the Egyptian Wisdom would be lost had it not been preserved by the work of those Greeks who went there for their higher education. Those noted Greeks, when initiated into the Egyptian Mysteries, learned with astonishment that the Earth is round and revolves round the Sun. They also learnt that the Sun moves north each year till it finally shines for weeks at the North Pole. For two thousand years the European scientists laughed at the gullibility of the Egyptian Masters, until they finally discovered what these Masters had known for thousands of years. As we advance in knowledge of the Fourth Dimension, concerning which the Masters knew so much, we see a new era dawning, and the absurd theories of physical science are dying.

We are returning to the border-line of the Spiritual World, which physical science ridicules as a mythical realm of superstition, a figment of the imagination.

Physical science has been forced to admit the influence of Cosmic Rays in controlling life, or mysterious showers of electronic energy, of magnetic fluids, radiated by the sun and distant stars.

The press of October 12, 1950, mentioned "Radio stars, invisible and mysterious, sending stations scattered all over the heavens, (that) were today at the National Academy of Sciences in New York by Sir Lawrence director of the Cavendish Laboratory, Cambridge University, England."

That long night that began in the 4th century A.D., is ending, and the day is dawning when the discredited astrologers will descend from their garrets, or rise from the gutters, to take their rightful place again as the Intelligent Teachers of the world. Then shall our children study that Cosmic Science of the Ancient Masters which has shown its students down through the ages the secrets of their own Being.

Chapter 16
Dormant Organs (C)

Some have said that Roger Bacon possessed the greatest mind produced during the Middle ages. That would not be saying much when it is known how severe Mind Control was in those days of the all-powerful Pope.

So Bacon saw the picture in a dim light. He imagined that some mysterious, external "medicine" was to be taken from WITHOUT. The Ancient Masters knew better. They knew that all lays WITH IN the body itself. Modern science asserts that "the glory and treasure of philosophers which completely rectifies the human body, lie in the Endocrine Glands." Man is what these glands make him. More error. That hard it seems for science to find the fundamentals

To a large extent, man's glands are what he makes them by his mode of living, and as his glands are influenced by the vibrations of the environment in which he lives and labors.

The Endocrine Glands do the best work they can under the conditions supplied by the master of the body.

When man supplies perfect conditions, the glands perform perfect work. They cannot refine beneficial products front blood that is polluted with poisonous elements which enter the body with air, drink and food.

The Endocrine Glands are the Master Chemists of the organism. Upon their products depends the activity of all the other glands, as they function in response to proper stimulation. The glands themselves receive their primal stimulus from what enters man's body and from the vibrations of his environment.

Science finds that the gonad (sex) glands control the ductless-gland-system. The gonads are the Life-Glands that produce the most refined and most vital fluid in the organism.

The gonads are also called the "destructive glands" because it is their function that perpetuates the race; and in the act of reproduction man sacrifices to no small degree his own vital force and substance.

The Thymus Gland is one of the Endocrine System. This gland, according to anatomists, is -- "A two-lobed body in the lower neck and upper thorax of an infant or of a young animal. It appears to be a true lymph-gland, and to have a hematopoietic (blood-making) function. It begins to waste away about the second year, and usually disappears about the end of the 13th year." -- Amer. Illus. Med. Dict. by Dorland, 8th ed., page 1006.

According to Doctor Charles W. Greene's work on Physiology, the thymus is a ductless gland the function of which "little is known." "Our ignorance (of the body) is profound," days Doctor Carrel. Greene continues:

"Important information has recently been yielded by the biological studies of Gudernatsch. He fed dried thymus to frog tadpoles with the result that growth was strongly stimulated, but metamorphosis was indefinitely delayed.

"Tadpoles fed ordinary food begin differentiation that leads to metamorphosis upon reaching a certain maximum size and age. But the thymus-fed tadpoles continue to grow beyond the normal size without showing any signs of differentiation." -- page 472.

While they were fed dried thymus gland material, the tadpoles remained tadpoles. They did not shed their tails and become frogs. They showed no signs of age. The rising and setting of the sun did not affect them. They continued to remain young tadpoles. Is this the secret of perpetual youth?

The thymus has been termed "The Gland of Youth." The term seems to be supported fully and literally by the evidence supplied. Some authorities assert that the thymus is most active at puberty, and then begins slowly to atrophy for some unknown reason, usually becoming dormant after the age of 20 or 21 in most cases. Why does man lose the use of the gland put in his body by God to keep him always young? There must be a reason. Biologists show that the thymus is super-sensitive to salt, and the eating of salty food causes the gland to atrophy. It seems to require from ten to twenty years in most cases for the salt-eating-habit to destroy the thymus.

It is known that salt damages the entire body. It has a tendency to absorb water, and draws the precious fluids from the cells, glands, and organs, causing them to atrophy. It cripples the lymphatic and endocrine systems, including the gonad glands, and causes general deterioration of the whole organism.

Thus do our evil habits destroy us. We do well to live 60 or 70 years, and yet our body is so perfectly made that biologists declare it is apparently intended to go on forever.

Cunningham's Text-Book of Anatomy, containing nearly 1600 pages, gives a most complete description of the thymus. It says:

"IN some new-born babies it weighs as little as 2 or 3 gm., in others as much as 15-17 gm. At puberty it may be difficult to find, or may weigh as much as 40 gm. After the age of fifty it may require careful dissection to discover, or may be quite large." -- page 1334.

The functions of the most complex organs of the body "still remain unknown" says Carrel (page 94). What is the purpose and function of the thymus? Modern science has no answer, except to assume that the gland seems to act as a "check valve" on the gonad glands.

When the thymus is removed in the case of small animals, the gonad glands are hastened to maturity and show greater functional activity than in animals whose thymus functions normally.

Physiologists assert that this may reveal one reason why the creative function in modern man has become largely a matter of lust and debauchery. The "check valve" on the gonads is dormant and they run wild, free of all restraint. Excessive sex indulgence follows, and the work of the "destructive glands" hurries man to the grave.

Experiments on thousands of rats show that when the thymus is removed, the animals mature prematurely, age rapidly, produce prolifically, and die long before their natural life-span has been attained. That description perfectly fits modern man, with his atrophied dormant thymus gland.

To the best of our knowledge, modern science has offered no serious suggestion as to why the early Biblical Patriarchs did not mature and produce off spring until they were a hundred years old or more. Does the secret lie in the thymus gland?

Adam was 130 when he begat Seth; Methuselah was 187 when he begat Lamech; and Lamech was 182 when he begat Noah. These men lived nearly a thousand years. Possibly the thymus, in its normal development and function, had much to do with the prolonged period of youth and the exceedingly long life that resulted.

We know so little about man as he was thousands of years ago, before he became a victim of debauchery and degeneration, that it would be foolish to attempt to describe him. Nor does it make sense to suggest that glands are put in man's body for no other purpose than to atrophy, degenerate, and lapse into dormancy.

When the thymus, the "check valve" to the sex glands, has been removed, or has become dormant, the resultant excessive stimulation of the gonads, causing excessive sex indulgence as shown in experiments on animals, seriously weakens the body, causing it to age rapidly, to decline into decrepitude, and to sink down in early death. Science is searching for serums to correct this condition. The theory of Bacon the some mysterious, external "medicine" must be taken from WITHOUT.

So little seems to be known concerning this and many other matters affecting man, that science is incompetent to offer any useful suggestions. Some biologists contend that the thymus may be aroused from its dormant state and activated by the higher emotions, the chief of which seems to be genuine love between those of the opposite sex. It seems reasonable that God may have so provided it. But this does not mean that lust or sexual indulgence must follow. It means 'the loving interchange of those harmonious vibrations between the male and female bodies that preserve health and promote longevity.

No matter where the investigation begins, we invariably arrive at the same place.

The "destructive glands" have been properly thus designated. Man cannot consume and expend his vital essence in lustful conduct, nor in the function of perpetuating the species, without paying the price by sacrificing a definite part of his own existence.

For in the day that thou eatest thereof, dying thou shalt die (*Genesis 2:17*).

Man is given the intelligence and the willpower to consider and choose between (1) self-denial and preservation, or (2) self-indulgence and destruction.

Chapter 17
Spiritual Chambers (A)

"The body is the Temple of God. Within it are certain vital centers that open into inner shrines. Using these centers as points of contact, the Life Force from the higher plane flows into the body. It is thru these centers that the God Force must flow to spiritualize man's various bodies before their resurrection can occur. By resurrection we mean the ultimate building up of a spiritual body within the physical by a process of gradually raising the vibrations of its particles to respond to the Key-note sounded by the Higher Self" (Curtiss in *Voice of Isis*).

It is unsound and unscientific to suggest "the ultimate building up of a Spiritual Body within the physical." The Spiritual Body is the Solar Body, the Life Body, and on the visible plane it dwells in the Earth Body, the material garment of the Solar Body. It is the Real Man, the Eternal Man.

An author, clever in. the use and arrangement of words, can ramble along and fill many pages with intriguing remarks. When we finish reading his book and take inventory to determine what practical benefit we have gained, we discover how authors engage in word-play that may interest and entertain the average reader, while giving him very little that enriches his mind. Usually these authors write about things which they do not understand themselves.

According to the Bible, the Kingdom of God is within Man (*Luke 17:21*). Then where shall we look for the Throne of God but in Man. Furthermore, the Bible says that the kingdom of God is not a place in space, but a state of the mind (*Romans 14:17*).

This Throne of God, according to the Ancient Masters, is the mysterious Chambers in the skull, about which modern science knows so little; and these are the Spiritual Centers of the Golden Bowl (Brain) (*Ecclesiastics 12:6*).

These Chambers are five in number, and the Sankhya doctrine informs us that the five senses of the average conscious man are the exteriorized products of these five corresponding spiritual centers, which are as follows:

1) Frontal sinus— A cavity in the frontal bone of the skull. 2) Sphenoid sinus — A cavity in the sphenoid bone of the skull. 3) Maxillary sinus — Largest of the five, and resembles a pyramid in shape. 4) Palatine sinus — A cavity in the orbital process of the palatine bone and opening into either the sphenoidal or a posterior ethmoidal sinus. 5) Ethmoidal sinus — This chamber consists of numerous small cavities occupying the labyrinth of the ethmoid bone, and in these cavities are situated the small, mysterious glands known in occult science as the Intellectual Organs.

The sinuses communicate directly or indirectly with the nasal cavity; and it is highly significant to observe that they receive the Breath of Life directly and unmodified as it flows to them thru the nose, and before any of the other air organs have a chance to select and absorb any substance from the spiritual stream of the Cosmos, charged with every known element.

The sinuses are lined with the mucous membrane extending into them from the nose, and to them rapidly spreads all disorders that affect the nose. They receive the full charge of all poisonous gases in the air.

During a cold in the head, the inflammation extends from the nasal mucous lining to that of the sinuses, causing such discomforts as frontal headaches (frontal sinus), pain in the cheek (maxillary sinus), pain between the eyes (ethmoidal sinuses), and deep seated pain at back of eyes (sphenoidal sinus). These aches and pains, indicating serious damage being done to these spiritual chambers, are caused by the poisonous air entering the nostrils. The air may be so slightly polluted that it fails to produce the reaction called the "simple cold." Thus begins the destruction of the vital spiritual centers of man while he is only an infant.

The mucous excretions of the lining of the maxillary sinus, in inflammatory conditions, fill up this sinus, as the orifice is at its uppermost part. Much of this mucus as cannot be blown out through the nose, remains in the sinus and gradually hardens, destroying the function of that spiritual chamber, the largest of the group.

Full recovery from ailments is a myth. Each one is a step down the ladder of degeneration to the grave lying at the bottom. If the illness is slight, that downward step is short. If severe, that downward step is longer.

Recoveries from each illness are only partial, regardless of how slight the illness may be.

As the sinuses superficially appear as nothing more than air chambers in the skull, medical art, ignorant of their true function, stupidly assumes that their purpose is to lend resonance to the voice. The voice organ is in the throat, not in the nose nor in the sinuses.

The small glands, the mysterious Intellectual Organs, located in the skull near the point where the nose joins the forehead, are activated by the Mental Spirit that enters thru the nostrils into the sinuses, and, in function, they coordinate and collaborate with the sinuses. This is the Chief Spiritual Intelligent Center of man. The sinuses and these small glands constitute the spiritual sense-centers that receive from the cosmic source the Higher Intelligence that is too subtle for contact by the five physical senses of conscious man.

This stream of Higher Intelligence, Mental Spirit, incessantly flows into the sinuses as man breathes, but it can produce no reaction, no effect, when the glands and sinuses are deficient and dormant.

In wild birds and beasts, and the wild, uncivilized, uncontaminated natives that have not been tainted and tinged with the so-called "blessings" of our grand civilization, as we stated in our work titled "Kingdom of Heaven", these spiritual centers are functionally developed, and science attempts to explain the uncanny intelligence of these creatures and these wild people by asserting that they are guided by "instinct." But what "instinct" is, science fails to explain.

No animal was made more complete and more perfect than man was in the beginning of his physical existence. He once possessed that peculiar power termed "instinct," and had it in a higher degree than it now appears in birds and beasts. He lost it because of ages of mind control and degeneration resulting from bad environment, bad air, and bad habits of living.

The delicate centers of Higher Intelligence reception are deterioritized, dormantized and rendered practically useless in civilized man by the deadly, destructive action of the poisonous gases that he inhales from infancy to old age, provided he lives that long.

Think it over; consider it well; for you are now in a new field so little known that it is not even recognized nor casually mentioned in any known literature extant.

Chapter 18
Spiritual Chambers (B)

"The (physical) mind is not so robust as the body. Mental diseases by themselves are more numerous than all other diseases combined. Hospitals for the insane are full to overflowing, and unable to receive all those who should be restrained" (Carrel, *"Man, The Unknown"* page 154).

The brain and nerves release man from his physical tomb of silence and darkness, and give him what little knowledge he has of his physical existence and his physical environment. When man loses physical consciousness, he is spiritually dead so far as his conscious contact with the physical world is concerned.

When man loses his spiritual consciousness, he is spiritually dead while physically alive, so far as his conscious contact with the spiritual world is concerned. Occult science teaches that Man's Air Organs are his spiritual centers: Those "certain vital centers that open into inner shrines."

The Cosmic Force, the Divine Essence that animatizes the body and intellectualizes the mind, contacts the earth in a subtle, invisible form known as Air — a substance very lightly regarded by science, yet so potent and important that it contains all the elements found in the earth and in the human body.

As this potent stream flows thru man's nostrils, a certain portion of it enters and activates the "inner shrines" of the Temple, situated in the Golden Bowl (Skull), and called "sinuses."

In civilization, this potent stream without which man would die in a few minutes, is poisoned beyond description by his works and inventions. Polluted air fills cities and homes, and dormantizes the nerves extending to the brain from the five sinuses, the "inner shrines."

As the function of smelling weakens and fails because polluted air has deteriorated and dormantized the nerves extending to the brain from the nose, so the spiritual function of the sinuses weakens and fails for the same reason, and man becomes dead so far as the spiritual world is concerned.

It is a fact well-known to hunters that dogs lose their keen sense of smell if kept in houses where people live, and breathe the same polluted air that ruins the psychic powers of civilized man.

Little children in this civilization, only two and three years old, usually have a stream of mucus flowing almost continuously from their nose. That is the work of polluted air.

Only a small portion of that mucus is generated in the nose. Ninety percent of it is generated in the suffering sinuses, the spiritual chambers, the vital "inner shrines." Air simply passes thru the nose, having much less time to poison and irritate the nose than it has to damage and ruin the sinuses. For when the poisoned air enters the sinuses, there must remain, as there is no outlet.

People suffer much with their nose during a cold, and some suffer more from irritation of the sinuses. The sinuses are so severely poisoned by polluted air early in life, that they are soon deteriorated to a state of total ruin, after which they trouble the victim no more. His marvelous spiritual chambers are now dead.

Parts of the body that are dead in a living man, no longer give him pain or discomfort. He is glad to have an aching tooth pulled so it will trouble him no more. The price he pays for this relief is a lost tooth. The price he pays for relief from sinus trouble is the loss of his spiritual senses.

Whether the Masters were aware of this particular matter is unknown, as no reference to it has been found in their writings. Perhaps in their day the great ocean of air had not been polluted by man's works and inventions as it has been in this "wonderful civilization" of fraud and corruption.

In rare instances it still occurs that surprising intelligence is exhibited by a child of perhaps five or six years of age, and the child is regarded as a prodigy. Modern science is unable to offer any logical explanation of this strange phenomenon. The "wise doctors" do not understand that this is a case where polluted air has not yet had time to deterioritize and dormantize the spiritual centers of that child, and it is able to contact and receive certain phases of the Higher Intelligence direct from the Cosmic Source.

It is only a matter of time until the polluted air will have done its destructive work, and the child that was once a prodigy will sink, in the realm of intelligence, to the level of the social pattern, the condition of the multitude. Civilized man has not only lost practically all his spiritual powers of contact with the spiritual world, but he is rapidly losing his physical powers of contact with the physical world.

Dr. Carrel declares that in New York State one person out of every twenty-two must be placed in an asylum at some time or other. In the whole of the United States the hospitals care for almost eight times more feeble-minded or lunatics than consumptives. He continues:

"In the whole country (USA), besides the insane, there are 500,000 feeble-minded. In addition, surveys made under the auspices of the National Committee for Mental Hygiene have revealed that at least 400,000 children are so unintelligent that they cannot profitably follow the courses of the public schools. In fact, the individuals who are mentally deranged are far more numerous. It is estimated that several hundred thousand persons, not mentioned in any statistics, are affected with psychoneuroses. These figures show how great is the fragility of the consciousness of civilized men."

We saw that man is dead to the physical world when his physical senses fail. He is likewise dead to the spiritual world when his spiritual senses fail. The polluted air that ruins his sense of smell, also ruins his spiritual senses and weakens his whole body while he is still but a child.

Thus does man's environment make him what he is. There is no escape from this sad fate, except to flee to the mountains and jungles. But who will exchange the so-called blessings of this civilization for the precious gifts of primitive man? According to occult science, the functions of inhalation and exhalation are analogous to the Great Fiery Breath of Universal Spirit, which eternally flows forth and returns. when it flows out, there appear all the manifestations of worlds, men, and the realms below man.

At the completion of each Grand Cycle, involving eons of time, the Great Fiery Breath sucks back into itself the divided and the differentiated; and all things recede and disappear in the Grand Cosmic Circle, Absolutism, the Eternal and Primal Source from whence they come, there to remain for renovation and purification, and to issue forth again at the dawning of the next Cosmic Day.

The Divine Essence, the Cosmic Force or whatever we choose to call the Great Cosmic Breath of Life, enters man's body thru the nostrils (*Genesis 2:7*), the only channel provided for that purpose, and passes on to the lungs, there to be absorbed by the blood stream and carried to every cell of the body, while that Force governs the body's involuntary functions thru the sub-conscious Mind — a power generated in the Five Spiritual Centers of the Sinuses.

This is the final function that the crippled Sinuses can perform, and when that fails, Somatic death follows.

Chapter 19
Damnation

Man is what his environment and education make him. These mold the thoughts and fix the beliefs that control his Mind. When we control the Mind, we control the Man. To that end your environment was built around you, and the scope of your education was prepared by the powers that rule our civilization. So well has this work been done, that all you are looking for now is more evidence to support what you already believe; and you call that searching for Truth.

According to the gospel Jesus, "Ye shall know the truth, and the truth shall make you free" (*John 8:32*). But that freedom has not come because truth has been kept from the people. Before man can understand the truth, he must learn to understand the un-truth his cunning rulers have led him to believe was the truth.

You are prepared for the truth by learning how you have been deceived. To aid you in your search of truth, we shall reveal the Light that went out when Christianity was born in the fourth Century.

Take your Bible and read the last nine verses of the last chapter of the book of Mark. Behold how the church, in the Black Fourth Century, wrote its own law that rules your life:

"He that believeth and is baptized shall be saved; but he that believeth but shall be damned" (*Mark 16:16*).

What are you to believe? You are to believe in:

1. A physical resurrection.
2. A posthumous judgment.
3. A vicarious atonement.
4. A heaven for the saved.

5. A hell for the unsaved.

The church destroyed the evidence of its nefarious work, so the world knows little of the cause of that long, black night in European civilization, so essential to the propagation of its Doctrine of Damnation.

The era began in the 4th Century A.D., when the epoch-making event occurred that changed the calendar of the Christian world and the entire course of Europe, Egypt, Asia Minor, and all countries ruled by the Roman Empire. Then rapidly followed many changes, including the destruction of ancient temples of science and religion, the burning of ancient scriptures and historic records, the persecution, liquidation and assassination of learned men — and the advent of the Dark Ages.

A history of that period could not be written due to the destruction of historic records, the ban on learning, and the suppression of knowledge. In fact, the church laid down the rule to govern its followers in this interpolation: "I am determined not to know anything among you, save Jesus Christ, and him crucified" (*1 Corinthians 2:2*).

The burning of the famous Alexandrian Libraries in Egypt by those bent on the destruction of ancient wisdom, caused the loss of most of the historic and scientific records of the ancient world.

From all parts of the globe the writings and discoveries of the Masters had been collected and deposited in several spacious buildings especially the Bruckion and Serapeum.

Thus the Sun of Ancient Science, which had lighted the path of the traveler from the days of Adam, was to sink in darkness and rise no more until distant generations would come to understand what the Masters had discovered concerning the mysteries of Man and Creation.

All Europe was fated to see and suffer the horrors of the blackest and most terrible night the world has ever known or ever will know. The ancient religion was now called "paganism" (heathenism) to discredit and make it appear revolting. Those who dared adhere to it, were smeared, and termed "heathens," and bitterly persecuted and put to death.

The church spread darkness and ignorance to conceal the fact that the old religion was based on the discoveries of Ancient Science covering thousands of years; while the new religion was invented in a convention of bishops in 325 A.D., and founded on fraud, as explained in our work titled "Mystery Man of the Bible." The old religion recognized a scientific law of animation and spiritualization. The new religion was divorced from all law and depended, and still depends, upon ignorance and superstition.

The old religion was based on the scientific principle that Birth in the physical world is Death in the Spiritual World, while Death in the physical world is Birth in the Spiritual World, as we have explained in our work titled "Cosmic Creation," in which we showed that Death is a creative process in every respect just as Birth is. The new religion is based on the absurd theory of a physical resurrection, a posthumous judgment, a vicarious atonement, a mythical heaven for the saved, and a mythical hell for the damned.

In that long night of terror and blood-shed, termed in history "religious wars," Heaven was invented and placed in the sky, and the fraud nurtured by the church, while it made man an ignorant coward and a cringing slave.

In the same way, Hell was invented and nurtured by the fears and servile fancies of deceived man during that dark period, when dungeons of torture were a recognized part of every European government; and God was depicted as an infinite tyrant, with infinite resources of vengeance (*Deuteronomy 32:35*).

Physical resurrection: In the gospel of Osiris, written ages before the Christian era, Osiris was the god-man who rose from the dead and lived in a body perfect in all its members. It did not decay like the bodies of other men; neither putrefaction nor worms acquired power over it; or caused it to diminish in the least degree. He was the resurrection, and could give life after death because he had attained it. He made men to be born again into the new and eternal life beyond the grave. He could give life because he was life; and he could make man to rise from the dead because he was the resurrection (*John 11:25*).

When the church revised certain passages in the Bible to make them support certain false dogmas, including the resurrection, it changed the following statement in Job: "Though after my skin this body be destroyed, yet without my flesh shall I see God" — to read: "And though after my skin worms destroy this body yet in my flesh shall I see God" (*Job 19:26*).

This materialistic conception of resurrection was interpolated in the Bible by the church to support its fraud of the literal resurrection of its Jesus. Thus throughout the Bible it made interpolations to support its fraudulent dogmas; and all the so-called prophecies were interpolated in the Bible after the events had come to pass.

1. Posthumous judgment: This theory was taken from the gospel of Osiris. He was the judge of men after death, and the arbiter of their future destiny. But it was necessary to obtain his favor by means of magical and religious words and ceremonies.

2. Vicarious atonement: Osiris, Krishna, Buddha, and all the ancient gods were "saviors of the world." Krishna was called "The savior of men."

The church prefixed the first nine verses to the first chapter of Revelation to make it appear as the "Revelation of Jesus Christ," who "washed us from our sins in his own blood," while it stupidly left in Galatians the Masters' philosophy, that "God is not mocked; for whatsoever a man soweth, that shall he also reap" (*Galatians 6:7*). For fifteen hundred years no one in a Christian country dared question the Church doctrine of Damnation, — except at the risk of his life.

The church kept the Bible away from the people, and it passed into comparative obscurity. Translations were made in secret for fear of the church, and the "reading of the Bible was prohibited by both church and state," says Professor Roswell D. Hitchcock (D.D., LL.D.) in his History of the Bible (page 1159). The first man in England who dared print the Bible in English, so people might read it and judge for themselves, was burned at the stake for "his impious act."

Servetus questioned the church doctrine, and was burned at the stake in 1553. Julius Vanninus of Italy was burned at the stake in 1619 for uttering "atheistic sentiments."

Bruno (1548-1600) disagreed with the church. He asserted the "pagan philosophy" of the Unity of God, the Universal Substance, the One and Only Principle. He said "That which is in things, and yet is distinct from them as the universal is distinct from the particular is the same." For voicing this "pagan principle" he was burned at the stake. Galileo (1564-1642) declared what the Masters well knew, that the earth is round and revolves around the Sun. He was cast into prison and forced to recant or be put to death.

Queen Isabella of Spain, writing to the bishop of Segovia of her efforts to promote Christianity and destroy the God Science of the Masters, said: "I have caused great calamities. I have depopulated towns and provinces and kingdoms (by having the people murdered) for the love of Christ and his holy mother" (*History of Inquisition*, page 124).

That is how the church triumphed. That is the way "Paganism," the Science of the Masters, was eradicated. There lies the basic cause of the Dark Ages.

In spite of these known facts of history, the Christians publish deception and fraud regarding the spread of Christianity. It was forced on the people by the church and state. To that end, the church destroyed all learning and the world's greatest empire. By the 13th century there was no civilization worthy of the name in all Christendom.

If the reader would know more about the Lost Wisdom of the Ancient Masters, he should read our other works on that subject as listed in the back of this folio.

Chapter 20
Science

The Sciences ... of Living Beings remain in a rudimentary state. ... Men of Science know not where they are going. ... The Science of Man is the most difficult of all Sciences. ... The Science of Man is still too rudimentary to be useful (*Man The Unknown,* pages 10, 23, 27, 179).

Thus speaketh Alexis Carrel, M.D., one of the truely great scientists of the present century.

It becomes increasingly evident, as we watch the "march of science," that if intelligent men do not destroy the system of MATERIALISM masquerading as Science, it will destroy them.

There are two systems of thought which pass as science. They lead in opposite directions, the one going inward and backward, and the other outward and forward. The former is called the Inductive Process; the latter, the Deductive Process.

Francis Bacon (1561-1626) and Auguste Comte (1798-1857) were the materialists who did the work that led to the founding of the Inductive System, which later became Modern Material Science.

The postulates and arguments of these two men profoundly influenced such researchers as Littre, Mill, Humboldt, Lewes, Grote, Darwin, Spencer, Wallace, Harrison, Huxley, Fiske, and other protagonists of the Evolution in what came to be called "The Wonderful Century" (19th) because so much was accomplished in that period in new discoveries and inventions.

The 19th century saw such a revolution of human thought that it seemed for a time that Spiritualism would be swept into the sea, and the Religionists trembled.

Material science rose to the status of a religion, and the Bible was regarded as the work of "superstitious heathens." Professor J. H. Woodger said: "Genesis is not in it with a school text-book on chemistry."

This dogmatism dates from the days of the materialists who imagined the Universe to be a vast machine made of hard, indivisible atoms. Thinking was just the vibration of molecules in the brain. Consciousness was an "epiphenomenon and everything progressed under the impact of the mechanical force of evolution.

The men who invented the Inductive System were guided by observation, by what they saw. We observe a certain number of facts and, on the grounds of analogy, extend what we think is true of them, to other facts of the same class, thus arriving, as we think, at general principles or laws. The pitfalls of this system rises from the fact that we usually see not what we think we see. It often happens that we see just the reverse; and for that reason the opinions and conclusions of the Intuitionists are faulty and misleading.

In the Deductive System, we begin with General Principles, and, on the grounds of analogy, seek to connect these with some definite case by means of a middle term of objects known to be equally connected with both. Thus we bring down the general to the individual, as the Ancient Masters did, affirming of the latter the distinctive qualities of the former, and asserting, as the Masters did, "As above, so below."

The Ancient Masters stated their system in these words: For the invisible things from the creation of the world are clearly seen (in the mind), being understood by the things that are made (visible) (*Romans 1:20*).

And, we look not (for guidance) at the things which are seen, but at the things which are not seen; for the things which are seen are temporal (fleeting, changeable, shadowy); but the things which are not seen are eternal (fixed, permanent) (*II Corinthians 4:18*).

The Inductions declares that his way is the only correct way of attaining to reliable knowledge. And it has even come to pass in modern times that no system is considered of any value except the Inductive. And no system could be more deceptive.

And so, physical science has extended the Inductive System for Creative Processes, and on to the human body and its functions, thus making medical art a precarious system of speculation and experimentation.

According to Inductive Science, the Universe is composed of blind and un-known forces, humanity is nothing but infinitely small particles on the surface of a grain of dust lost in the immensity of the cosmos, and this cosmos is totally deprived of life and consciousness. Our universe is exclusively mechanical.

Concerning this conclusion of Inductive Science, Professor A. N. Whitehead wrote:

"The old foundations of scientific thought (based on observation) are be-coming unintelligible. Time, space, matter, material, ether, electricity, mechanism, organism, configuration, structure, pattern, function — all require reinterpretation. What's the sense of talking about a mechanical explanation, when we do not know what we mean by mechanics" (*Science and the Modern World*).

The Inductive Scientists are lost in an inextricable jungle because they have missed and omitted the great Central

Factor which would explain all had it been discovered, recognized and included. But that Great Central Factor, according to Inductive Science, has no existence beyond the imagination of the Deductive Scientists. Every way we turn, we find ourselves passing and reposing these bewildered Intuitionists, who are constantly trying this way and that in the hope of reaching the goal of their ambition.

We leave them in their confusion, start with a self-existent General Principle, and by logical steps and consistent strides, bring it down from the general to the individual, leaving no gaps to be bridged and no gulfs to be crossed. We shall move the Macrocosm down to the Microcosm, the Celestial to the Terrestrial, and affirm of the latter all the distinctive qualities of the former, in agreement with the Ageless Wisdom of the Ancient Masters who said, "As above, so below," as the Creator, so the Created.

Under the Law of Sameness that Like begets Like, it could not be otherwise; and that position is so factual and conclusive that the Biblical Makers declare, "God created man in his own image and likeness" (*Genesis 1:26, 27*). At this vital point we must proceed with care and caution, strictly observing the philosophy of the Ancient Masters who said, "God is Spirit" (*John 4:24*).

We should not let a God pop up in our mind as a great man with a flowing white beard, sitting on a throne, with a scepter in one hand and a globe in the other, as pictured in literature for children and the child mind.

In due time and proper form we shall dissipate the fog and ignorance concerning God by presenting Him in His cosmic costume and cosmic character. We shall do this by consistently proceeding forward and outward, from the Cosmic Unity at the center to a marvelous Variety at the surface, and declare and show that the Masters had the facts and understood the facts when they phrased their great maxim, "As above, so below." From an invisible center to a visible manifestation is the order of Creation, without an exception in the Universe, and unconsciously admitted by both the Materialists and Evolutionists, who acknowledge a Great First Cause as Infinite and Absolute, and by the Religionists by asserting, "The Kingdom of God is within you." (*Luke 17:21*). Where would God be if not in His Kingdom?

These two systems of science are both said to be based on facts. The great difference lies in the facts not being the same class of facts. The Deductive System bases all practice and procedure on a Central Cause (as the seed), which contains within itself all that is, was, or ever will be. The Inductive begins at the surface and gets lost in confusion as it attempts to trace effects in searching for the Central Cause.

In both cases, reasoning is assumed to precede practice; but the postulate from which the reasoning proceeds differs as Cause and Effect.

All observable facts are the Effects of a Cause. The Cause that proceeds, being discovered, constitutes an eternal verity, a general principle, which changes not, and so, becalms the fixed foundation from which reasoning is conducted by the Deductionist in a regular, consistent, forward and outward process, thru infinite time to infinite results. Such process is natural, reasonable, logical, cosmical, scientific, and consistent with all the Creative Processes of the Universe.

Reasoning from facts observed, as the Inductive Scientists do, is an unnatural, unscientific, illogical, illusive, and deceptive course; for – he saw with his own eyes the Moon is round; Was equally sure the Earth was square, as he'd travelled fifty miles, and found no sign that it was circular anywhere. – Doctor Robert Walter.

Inductive Scientists reason not from facts, but from what they observe. And what they observe is most often an illusion, and usually the reverse of the facts. And so, it is not strange nor surprising that medical art and physical science, based upon observation, are constantly "progressing" from one fallacy to another.

Physical science reasons from an assumption arising from an illusion of observation, and the conclusion cannot be more reliable than the premise. For every conclusion is an evolution of its postulate, just as certainly as every plant is an evolution of its seed.

Cosmic Science of the Ancient Masters is, and must be, the unfolding of universal principles, corresponding to the evolution of every living organism, as the bloom of the flower is the evolution of the bud. Creation in all cases, whether of a universe, a world, a living thing, a man, or a science of thought, is an evolution, an unfolding of an Invisible Principle which, actually existent holds within itself the promise and potency of all that follows. Scientific reasoning proceeds from Cause to Effect, from seed to fruit, from Principle to Product, corresponding to all Cosmic Processes. Such reasoning reduces the complexity of the Universe to the simplicity of science. The products of Creation are multifarious, even beyond human comprehension, but Causes, on the contrary, are few in number, simple in character, and certain in operation. Having discovered the Cause of any class of phenomena, we have attained to a certainty of knowledge which contrasts gloriously with the confusing assumptions and speculations of Inductive Science.

All Principles are Causes, all Causes are Forces, and all Forces always function according to definite laws, as the rising of the Sun and the falling of the rain. And not only as to the Universe, but equally certain as to the human body. To reduce the complexities of Creation to the simplicities of science involves, primarily, a discovery of the Law which, rising from the operation of its corresponding force, explains all mysteries as to the phenomena of every class. Such a system of science is deductive, logical, certain, exact, and is based upon Universal Law. A Principle is a force that operates according to law; and it has always been the discovery of the Law of Operation in all ages that imparts certainty and exactness to science.

When we have discovered the Law involved in all cosmical and vital phenomena, we can formulate the Law of Creation. And when that is done, it will reveal the illusive, deceptive character of the conclusions of physical science as to the quality, quantity, essence and source of the mysterious state called Life.

This drawing of the Four Horsemen, made by Albrecht Darer in 1500, was based on the grim prophecy of Revelations 6:8: "And power was given unto them to kill with the sword, and with hunger, and with death."

The Bible is a Mystery

God's wisdom in a mystery, even the wisdom that hath been hidden — *1 Corinthians 11:7*.

"And ye shall know the truth, and the truth shall make ye free." — *St. John 8:32*.

"If there is one among You who is deficient in wisdom, let him pray to the spirit of truth, who comes to the simple-minded, but does not obtrude upon any one, and he will surely obtain it." — Jacob Epist. verse 5.

"Call unto me, and I will answer thee, and spew thee great and mighty things." – *Jeremiah Chapter 33*.

"Hear, O my son, and receive my sayings, and the years of thy life shall be many. I have taught thee in the ways of wisdom; I have led thee in the right paths. When thou guest, thy steps shall not be straitened, and when thou runnest, thou shalt not stumble. TAKE FAST HOLD OF THE INSTRUCTION let her not go; keep her, for she is thy life." — *Proverbs 4:10-13*.

"Stand in awe and sin not."

"Commune with your own heart upon your bed and be still." — *Psalm 4:4*.

"The Spirit searcheth all things, yea, the deep things of God." — *I Corinthians 2:10*.

"What man knoweth the things of a man, save the spirit of man, which is in him even so the things of God knoweth no man, but the Spirit of God." — *I Corinthians 2:2*.

I was dead; but behold, I live again.

If you succeed, praise God and Be Silent.

"I sought and found; I purified (it) often, I mixed (it) and caused (it) to mature. The golden tincture was the result; it is called the center of nature; The origin of all thought, and of all the books of men and various fogies. I now acknowledge freely, it is a panacea. For all the metals, the weak ones (in the constitution of man), And a point which originated from God." — Harmannus Datichius, Anth. Famulus.

To him that overcomes, I will give him a white Stone, and in the stone a new name written, which no man knoweth, saving he that received it. — *Revelation 2:17*.

Chapter 21
What Is Life

Hippocrates (460 B.C.) so- called Father of Medicine, said Life is a Flame burning in water. The human body is approximately 80% fluid.

Modern science has been unable to determine what Life is. It even denies the existence of Life as a cosmic Principle. It regards Life as an expression of physicochemical action. Wm. Osler, greatest physician America ever produced wrote:

"The studies of physiologists and physiological chemists abundantly indicate that all vital activities are ultimately the expression of molecular rearrangements and combinations. Therefore, Life is the expression of a series of chemical changes, and the material endowed with Life must be of such a nature that it is composed of molecules which react" (Mod. Med. 1907, page 39).

Osler's description of Life is merely a reference to certain signs of vital activity; of the manifestation of Life. The definition of Life must comprehend the element attested. It must explain the cause of the changes mentioned by Osler, or it is not a definition of Life, but a description of the effects or manifestation of the activity of Life. In his remarkable book, *"Man the Unknown,"* one of the great scientists of this century, Doctor Alexis Carrel, referred to the physicochemical conception of Life described by Osler as "childish" (page 108). But that is the theory of Life taught in medical books and medical schools and observed by the Medics.

In the Magic Book of Life called the Bible it appears that the great Pythagorean philosopher, Apollonius, called Paul in the Bible, made a definite effort to define the cosmic

Principle Life. We shall repeat what he said, according to the Bible: --

Some man will say, How are the dead raised up? and with what body do they come? Thou fool, that which thou sowest is not quickened, except it die: And that which thou sowest, thou sowest not that body which shall be, but bare grain, it may chance of wheat, or of some other grain.

All flesh is not the same flesh. There is one kind of flesh of men, another flesh of beasts, another of fishes, and another of fowls. There are also celestial bodies, and bodies terrestrial; but the glory of the celestial is one thing, and the glory of the terrestrial is another.

There is a natural (terrestrial) body, and there is a spiritual (celestial) body. And so it is written, the first man Adam was not that which is Spiritual but that which is natural; and afterward that which is spiritual

The first man is of the earth, earthy; the second man is the Lord from heaven. As the earthly, such are they also that are earthy, and as is the heavenly, such are they also that are heavenly. And as we have borne the image of the earthy, we shall also bear the image of the heavenly.

Behold, I show you a mystery: We shall not sleep, but we shall be changed, in a moment, in the twinkling of an eye, at the last trump; for the trumpet shall sound, and the dead (spirit in the body) shall be raised (out of the body) incorruptible, and we shall be changed (from terrestrial to celestial bodies). For we know that if our earthly house of this tabernacle were dissolved, we have a building of God, a house not made with hands, eternal in the heavens (*I Corinthians 15:35-55; II Corinthians 5:1*).

Has it ever been noticed that Paul here enumerates the four kingdoms on which man's existence rests at its corners, matching the four figures in Egyptology, and in Ezekiel's and John's celestial vision? Man, animal, fowl, fish.

The 15th chapter of I Corinthians marks the high point of spiritual sublimity reached in the New Testament. Its oracular grandeur should have lifted the body of Christian theology far above the mists of controversy that overhang it relative to the question of the corporeal resurrection.

But the later formulators of orthodox theology looked askance at Paul and classed him as a heretic. They would have ousted his Epistle from the canon if they had dared.

Paul's definition of Life as the Lord from Heaven still leaves us in darkness as to the actual nature of Life. Let us look at this mystery from another angle. If we lift the brain out of the body, nothing is left but a mass of dead flesh and bone. Paul's assertion as to Life fails to agree in any way with the theory of science. His observation that life is the Lord from heaven is symbolical. But it indicates that, in his opinion, Life is an eternal Principle.

The Bible says that God formed man of the dust of the ground, and breathed into his nostrils the BREATH OF LIFE; and man became a living soul (*Genesis 2:7*).

That is a fabulous statement, but we know that living is breathing. When we stop breathing we stop living. Even hibernating animals, sleeping all winter, must have air or perish. And so this evidence proves that the Life Principle exists in the air.

In 1643 John Mayow discovered in the air an element he called Spiritus Nitraerius. He said:

"In respiration an aerial element essential to Life passes into the blood. These vital particles having been extracted by the blood from the air in the lungs, the air expelled by the lungs is unfit to breathe again."

This discovery by Mayow meant so little to medical science, that it was not even noticed for a century. The secret of Life seemed to have no interest for the Holy Medical Hierarchy. No doubt there was a secret reason. The same old game of keeping the common cattle in ignorance and darkness in order to keep them in slavery. In 1774 Priestly rediscovered Mayow's Spiritual Nitroaerius, and isolated a gas he called Oxygen. In 1782 Lavoisier expounded what Oxygen is, thus throwing more light on the Life Function, but failing to find the secret of Life. Then in the middle of the 19th century Dr. Gustav Magnus of Germany proved the presence of gases in the blood. And for the first time in medical history the vital function of respiration began to assume a definite form. But the Life Principle becomes active in the body before the lungs are formed and before breathing begins. To solve this secret, we must go way back beyond books. For no author in modern times has noticed it in any book we have ever found.

The seed-cell in the mother's body that is the beginning of a baby is independent of the mother. It's not subject to her vital force. The vital force that energizes the seed-cell of the baby is the beginning of Life of the baby. And that force comes from the same cosmic source as that of the mother.

The source of that force which is the beginning of Life in man is unknown to modern science. It's another one of Creation's mysteries. At last some of these mysteries are being understood. Some of the mystery surrounding this point was recently dispelled by the discovery of certain scientists. According to the press of June 1, 1957, this discovery related to an invisible radar beam.

According to the account, two doctors, working on radar development during World War II, were surprised to find that in less than a minute invisible radar beans can kill a person.

In 10 seconds a technician in an electronic plant in Los Angeles, standing in the beam of a radar transmitter, felt sensations of heat in his abdomen. In less than a minute the heat made him move out of range of the rays. Within 15 days the man died. The surface of his body showed no signs of injury, but, according to the report, "his insides were cooked. a hole as big as a silver dollar had been burned in his small bowel." The doctors said that micro-waves emitted by a radar transmitter can pierce the walls of a building and cause intolerable heat to the body. This is an important discovery. It appears to reveal the mystery of the Silver Cord mentioned in the Bible (*Ecclesiastics 12:6*). The Ancient Masters must have had knowledge of micro-waves, but little of the information has come down to us.

The brain is the first organ formed in the baby. If we lift the brain out of the body, nothing is left but a mass of dead flesh and bone. If a blow to the head knocks you unconscious, you are the same as dead. Yet you breathe and your heart beats. But you have no sensations and feel nothing. If a big knife were plunged thru your body, you would not know it or feel it. Then you regain consciousness. From the apparent dead state you return to the living state. What has happened? Nothing except your brain recovered from the effect of the blow that knocked you unconscious and began to function normally.

The brain is just a mass of matter. How can it bring you to the living state from the apparently dead state? There's a great secret involved here that is not expounded in the books. Paul may have known it, but he did not mention it.

The Bible fails to identify the Silver Cord. But now we know from facts observed and facts inferred that it is related to the invisible radar beam that scientists recently discovered, which has such a powerful effect on the body, as mentioned in our folio titled *"The Flame Divine."*

The Silver Cord must be the cosmic link between the celestial and terrestrial bodies. It penetrates the brain and gives it the power called Life. And so, when the brain is in condition to function normally, the body is filled with Glorious Life.

This knowledge reveals the nature of Consciousness. The evidence indicates that it is brain function. And brain function results from power received from the Spiritual World thru the Silver Cord. That power appears to be the Spiritus Nitroaerius discovered by Mayow in 1643.

What is Consciousness? We've searched thru the books for sixty years to learn that secret but never found any reasonable answer. In his big book of 1014 pages, published in 1946, Professor H. W. Percival related unusual data as to Consciousness. He wrote:

"Consciousness is the ultimate, the final Reality. It's that by the presence of which all things are conscious. Mystery of all mysteries, it's beyond the comprehension. Without it, nothing can be conscious; no one could think; no being, no entity, no force, no unit, could perform any function. Yet, Consciousness itself performs no function. It does not act in any way; it's just a presence, everywhere. And it's because of its presence that all things are conscious in whatever degree they are conscious."

Percival appeared not to know what we have related, showing that Consciousness is one of the functions of the brain. And brain function results from power received from the Spiritual World thru the Silver Cord. Now, what is Life? The Life of the human body appears as the effect of vital force received from the cosmic source thru the Silver Cord, according to the evidence.

Chapter 22
How Gods Are Born

Doctor James Clark, of London, an exceptionally wise man, said, in his book, "Eternal Time," that god made man, and then man began making gods and has never stopped." Then he added: "The atomatic agencies of the Universe that created the sun, moon and stars, also created gods and angels, ghosts and devils, monkeys and men."

To find the gods and goddesses of our ancient ancestors, we must look to the forms and forces of Creation. The sun, the moon, the planets, the stars, the sky, the sea, the earth, the night, the dawn, the clouds, the wind, the storm, the thunder and lightning, rain, seasons, vegetation, etc. It's now an established fact that these were personified and worshipped in the temples.

The words that denoted these forms and forces would signify living things and living persons. And from personification to deification, the steps would be short, and the cunning priests would attend to that. All the expressions that had been attached to living forces and natural formations would remain as the description of personal and anthropomorphic gods. Every word would become an attribute and all thoughts, once grouped around a simple object, would branch off into distinct personifications. Naturally, the glorious Sun was the lord of light, the driver of the chariot of the day, and he toiled for the sons of man. Then, in the evening, he sank down to rest after a hard battle. Then the lord of light would be Phoebus Apollo, while Helios would remain enthroned in the fiery chariot, and his toils and earthly struggles would be transferred to Hercules.

The violet clouds which greeted his rising and his setting would now be represented by herds of cattle which feed in earthly pastures. There would be many other expressions which would still remain as floating phrases and attached to any of the deities. These would gradually be converted by the priests into incidents in the life of the heroes, and woven at length into systematic narratives. Finally, these gods, or heroes, and the incidents of their mythical careers would each receive a local habitation and a name. And the priests would see that these remained as real history after the origin and meaning of the words had either been wholly or partially forgotten.

For proof of these assertions, we have only to examine the Vedic poems, which furnish indisputable evidence that such as this was the origin and development of Babylonian and Egyptian mythology. In these poems the names of most of the gods indicate natural objects which, if endowed with life, have been transformed to human personality. In the poems, Eos is still the goddess of the dawn. As morning twilight appears, she rises from the couch of her spouse, Tithonus, and ascends in a Chariot drawn by horses from the River Oceanus, which encircles the world, to herald the splendor of the new born sun.

The cattle of Helios are still in the light-colored clouds which dawn leads out into the pastures of the sky. There the idea of Hercules has not yet been separated from the image of the toiling sun, and the glory of the life-giving Helios has not been transferred to the god of Delos and Pytho.

In the Vedas the myths of Endymion, of Kephalos and Prokris, of Orpheus and Eurydike, are exhibited in the form of detached mythical phrases, which furnish for each their germ.

This analysis could be extended indefinitely, but the conclusion can be only that in the Vedic terminology appears the foundation not only of the legends of Hellas, but of the somber mythology of the Scandinavian and the Teuton. Both have grown up largely from names grouped around the sun. But the former has been grounded on those expressions which describe the recurrence of day and night, and the latter on the great tragedy of nature, in the alternation of summer and winter.

Of this vast mass of solar myths, some have emerged into independent legends, others have furnished the foundation of whole epics, and others have remained simply as floating tales whose intrinsic beauty no poet has wedded in his verse. The evidence obtained from an examination of language in its several forms, leaves no room for any doubt that the general system of mythology has been traced to its fountain-head.

In spite of the clever work of the priesthood, we can no longer close our eyes to the fact that there was a stage in the history of speech, during which all the abstract words in common use today were utterly unknown; when men had formed no notion of virtue or prudence, of thought and intellect, of slavery and freedom, but spoke only of the man who was strong, who could point out the way to others and choose one thing out of many; of the man who was not bound to anyone, and was able to do as he pleased.

That even this stage was not the earliest in the history of language is the growing opinion among philologists. But for the comparison of legends, current in different countries, it's unnecessary to carry the search any further back. Speech without words denoting abstract qualities implies a condition of thought in which men were only awakening to a sense of the objects which surrounded them, and points to a time when the world was to them full of strange sights and sounds, some beautiful, some bewildering, some terrific, when, in short, they knew little about themselves beyond the vague consciousness of their existence and little of the phenomena of the external world.

In such a state, men could but attribute to all that they saw, or touched, or heard, a life which was like their own in its consciousness, its pleasure, and its sufferings; and they were right. That power of sympathizing with nature, which we are apt to regard as a special gift of the poet, was then shared by all.

This sympathy was not the result of any effort. It was natural and inseparably connected with the words which rose to their lips. It implied no special purity of heart or mind; it pointed to no mythical paradise, where shepherds knew not how to wrong or oppress or torment one another.

We say the light of the rising sun rests on the mountains; they said the sun was greeting his bride as naturally as our own poet would speak of the sunlight as clasping the earth, or the moonbeams as kissing the face of the sea.

We have then a stage of speech corresponding to a stage in the history of the human mind in which all sensible objects were regarded as being endued with conscious life. The varying phases of that life were described as factually as they described their own feelings of pleasure or suffering; and hence every phase became a picture. So long as the condition of their life remained unchanged they knew what that picture meant and ran no risk of confusing one with another. Then they had but to describe the things they saw, felt, or heard, in order to keep an inexhaustible store of phrases describing the facts of the world from their point of view. This language was the natural result of observation not less keen than that by which the inductive philosopher extorts the secrets of the natural world; nor was its range much narrower.

Each object received its own measure of attention, and no one phenomenon was so treated as to leave no room for others in their turn. They could not fail to observe the changes of days and years, of growth and decay, of winter and summer, of calm and storm. But the objects which so changed were to them living things. And the rising of the sun and its setting, the return of winter and summer, the growth and decay of vegetation, became a drama of Creative Action in which the actors were either their enemies or their friends.

That this is a logical review of the facts in the history of the human mind, philology alone would prove. But not a few of these phrases have come down to us in their earliest form and point to a long-buried stratum of language of which they are the fragments.

These relics exhibit in their germs the myths that later became the legends of the gods and heroes with human forms, and furnished the foundation of the epic poems of the world.

The mythical language of ancient man had no partialities. And if the career or the Sun occupies a large extent of the horizon, we cannot fairly simulate ignorance of the cause. Men so placed would not fail to put into words the thoughts and emotions aroused in them by the varying phases of that mighty globe on which we, no less than they, feel that our very life depends. And proof of this is easily found in the fact that the face of the earth would become like a barren rock if the Sun should set and never rise again.

Thus developed a multitude of expressions which described the Sun as the ghost of the night, as the destroyer of the darkness, as the lover of the dawn — of phrases which would go on and speak of the Sun as killing the dew with his spears, and of forsaking the dawn as he rose in the heavens.

The fact that the fruits and flowers of the earth were called forth by the warmth of the Sun could find expression in words which spoke of him as the friend and benefactor of man; while the constant recurrence of his work would lead men to describe him as a being constrained to toil for others, as deemed to travel over many lands, and as finding everywhere things on which he could bestow his love or which he might destroy with his power. Again, his journey might be across cloudless skies or amid alternations of calm and storm. His light might break fitfully through the dark clouds, or be hidden for many weary hours, or burst forth at last with glowing splendor as he sank down in the western sky. He would then be described as facing many dangers and enemies, but none of whom were able to arrest his course.

Then as the veil was rent at eventide, they would speak of the chief who had long remained still, girding on his armor; or of a wanderer throwing off his disguise and seizing his bow or spear to smite his foes; of the invincible warrior whose face shone with the flush of victory when the fight is finished, as he greets the fair-haired Dawn who closes the day as she began it.

To the wealth of the images thus lavished upon the daily life and death of the Sun, there would be hardly any limit. He was the child of the morning, the warrior of the day, and the victor of the night. And so with the various sights and sounds in nature. The darkness of night produced a feeling of vague honor and dread, and the return of daylight cheered them with a sense of gladness. And thus the Sun who scattered the black shades of night would be the mighty champion doing battle with the beast that lurked in its dark hiding place.

As the Sun performed his journey day by day through the tract less heavens, the state of the seasons is changed. The buds and blooms of spring-time appear and expand into flowers and fruits of summer, and on the approach of winter the leaves wither and fall. Thus, the daughter of the earth would be regarded as dying or as dead, as severed from her mother during the weary winter months, not to be restored to her again until the time for her to return from the dark land when spring-time would once more arrive.

As no other power but that of the Sun can resurrect dead vegetation to life, this child of the earth would be represented as buried in sleep from which the touch of the Sun alone could arouse her, when he says the frost and cold which lie as snakes around her motionless form.

These phases of nature would furnish the germs of myths or legends teeming with human feeling. As soon as the meaning of the phases were wholly or partially forgotten, it was inevitable that in the infancy of the race, man should attribute to all sensible objects the same kind of life which he himself was conscious of possessing. And our vaunted science has produced no evidence to show that they were wrong in the matter of Life. When we turn to the Bible, we find the Book of Psalms, which is nothing more than a song-book of praise of the various phases of Creation, much of which is devoted to the Sun.

But the priests invented a terminology in their effort to lead the uninformed mind away from the Sun and to their mythical God. We quote:

"O, clap you hands, all ye people; shout unto God with the voice of triumph. For the Lord (Sun) most high is terrible; he is a great King over all the earth." *(Psalms 47:1, 2)*.

"It is a good thing to give thanks unto the Lord, and to sing praises unto thy name, O most High. To show forth thy loving-kindness in the morning, and thy faithfulness every night." *(Psalms 92:1, 2)*.

"The Lord reigneth; let the earth rejoice; let the multitude of isles be glad thereof. Clouds and darkness are round about him, righteousness and judgment are the habitation of his throne. A fire goeth before him, and burneth up his enemies round about. His lightning's enlightened the world; the earth saw, and trembled. The hills melted like wax at the presence of the Lord of the whole earth. The heavens declare his righteousness, and all the people see his glory." *(Psalms 97:1-6).*

AND THE CIRCLE ROUNDS
Slowly the sun heralds morning,
The voice of a new day sounds,
Night covers atomic warning,
And the Cosmic circle rounds.
— Lee Richard Hayman.

1969 If a man die, shall he live again? Is reincarnation a fact? the sublime truths of the Universe. The Mysteries of Nature, of Man; the Grand cycle of Creation; Conscious & subconscious Mind; Intuition: Immortality; dormant Organs; The Mysterious chambers in the Skull. One of the great classics.

"The Lord reigneth; let the earth rejoice; let the multitude of isles be glad thereof. Clouds and darkness are round about him, righteousness and judgment are the habitation of his throne. A fire goeth before him, and burneth up his enemies round about. His lightning's enlightened the world; the earth saw, and trembled. The hills melted like wax at the presence of the Lord of the whole earth. The heavens declare his righteousness, and all the people see his glory." *(Psalms 97:1-6)*.

AND THE CIRCLE ROUNDS
Slowly the sun heralds morning,
The voice of a new day sounds,
Night covers atomic warning,
And the Cosmic circle rounds.
— Lee Richard Hayman.

1969 If a man die, shall he live again? Is reincarnation a fact? the sublime truths of the Universe. The Mysteries of Nature, of Man; the Grand cycle of Creation; Conscious & subconscious Mind; Intuition: Immortality; dormant Organs; The Mysterious chambers in the Skull. One of the great classics.